107 SHORT HUMOROUS STORIES FOR SENIORS

*Funny Easy-to-Read Stories to Reignite Memories, Stir Up
Nostalgia and Spark Conversation (Large Print)*

TENLEE GRAHAM

CONTENTS

FOREWORD

If you take your daily activities too seriously you will miss out on the humor life has to offer. These short stories are meant to remind you of when this happened to you, or you were involved in the activity. Do you have memories of something funny that happened to you while doing it? Think of the fun memories you have from all of the mundane activities of daily life. Reminisce with those who were involved with you or tell your story to your grandchildren. All of your past humanizes you, and the stories will connect you to others through this humanity. Think back and understand how rich your past was and the stories you can tell now.

Sincerely.

Tenlee Graham

In remembrance of my lovely first Grandson.
Grandma loves you always!

INTRODUCTION

Have you ever found yourself chuckling over the peculiarities that laced the golden years? For example, a simple family dinner can morph into an unscheduled comedy hour, or a misplaced pair of glasses can turn into a full-blown detective saga. Welcome to the world of seniors, where laughter bubbles over the rims of life's little moments, turning the mundane into a rich tapestry of memories and joy.

As someone deeply passionate about sprinkling dashes of happiness into the daily lives of seniors, I've always believed in the power of a good story —stories that not only tickle the funny bone but also light up the corridors of memory with a warm, nostalgic glow. That's why I've poured my heart and soul into curating this collection of 107 short humorous stories, each crafted to resonate with the beautiful, sometimes chaotic, tapestry of family life as seen through the eyes of seniors.

Why, you might ask? Beyond laughter, these stories are about connection. They're about bridging the generational gaps, knitting families closer with threads of shared laughter and understanding. In a world where the young and the old often find themselves on opposite ends of the technological and cultural spectrum, what better way to come together than over tales that speak a universal language of joy?

With a careful selection of themes and narratives, this book is designed to be a beacon for seniors. It is a light-hearted, engaging read that not only entertains but also engages the mind, stirring up those delightful waves of nostalgia while celebrating the wisdom that comes with age. And because we want this journey to be as comfortable as possible, we've ensured that each of these stories is presented in large print because squinting should be reserved for skeptical looks over dubious recipes, not for reading.

As we embark on this journey through time, from the laugh-out-loud absurdities of adapting to modern gadgets to the timeless warmth of family reunions, I invite you to anticipate each story. Imagine the joy of recognizing a piece of your own history in these pages, the comfort in knowing that you're not the only one who finds today's technology akin to alien wizardry.

Here is a brief anecdote that perfectly encapsulates the spirit of this book. The other day, I was attempting to explain to my neighbor, an endearingly stubborn octogenarian, how video calls work. Halfway through, she waved her hand dismissively and declared, "In my day, if we wanted to see someone's face when we talked to them, we just opened our front doors!" This delightful mix of wisdom, resistance to change, and humor is the essence of what you'll find in these pages.

Thank you, dear reader, for joining me on this adventure. It is with open arms and a heart full of gratitude that I welcome you into this collection of stories. They are more than mere words; they invite laughter, reflection, and shared joy. So, dive in, chuckle, reminisce, and remember to share the laughter with those around you. Who knows?

These stories are the perfect conversation starters for your next family gathering.

Welcome to "107 Short Humorous Stories for Seniors." Let the laughter commence!

CHAPTER 1

In the vibrant tapestry of senior living, few events sparkle with as much anticipation and collective eagerness as Senior Discount Day. It's a day that beckons with the promise of savings, a touch of adventure, and, perhaps, a sprinkle of unintended comedy. Amid the corridors of malls and the digital landscapes of online shopping, seniors navigate these opportunities with a blend of wisdom, excitement, and a keen eye for bargains. Yet, it's not merely the discounts that color these excursions but the rich, often humorous experiences that unfold along the way.

THE MISADVENTURES OF SENIOR DISCOUNT DAY

Unexpected Bargains

On a bright Tuesday morning, with the sun casting its warm glow over the bustling streets, a group of seniors found themselves at a local diner renowned for its Senior Discount Day. With menus in hand and conversations buzzing about the latest community news, the anticipation for a hearty meal at a fraction of the cost was palpable. However, confusion arose when the waiter, in a mix-up as delightful as it was unforeseen, applied the toddler's meal deal to their orders instead. The result was a fascinating array of miniature dishes, from tiny pancakes to petite cups of coffee, evoking laughter and amusement all around. This unexpected turn of events transformed their regular outing into a memorable one, where the small portions became a reminder of the joy found in life's little surprises.

Identity Confusion

During one such Senior Discount Day, an incident unfolded that would ripple through the community with chuckles and shared glances. In the quest to secure a deserved discount, a distinguished senior found herself in a humorous misunderstanding. While presenting her ID to a cashier, a bystander's offhand comment likened her to a well-known celebrity, much to the amusement of those around her. This case of mistaken identity, innocent and as fleeting as it was, sparked a series of jests and playful banter, casting a light-hearted mood over the proceedings. The incident highlighted the communal spirit of these outings. It served as a gentle reminder of the universality of aging, where wrinkles tell the stories of laughter, perseverance, and life's serendipitous moments.

Technology Troubles

In an era where technology increasingly mediates our experiences, senior discount adventures have also found a new battleground: the online world. A tale comes to mind of a senior attempting to navigate an e-commerce website armed with determination and a discount code. The challenge, however, wasn't securing the discount but warding off the myriad of online distractions and misleading advertisements. The ordeal ended with accidentally purchasing a gadget meant for the tech-savvy youth, leaving our protagonist bewildered yet amused. This escapade into the digital shopping realm serves as a testament to the resilience and adventurous spirit of seniors willing to traverse the complexities of technology for the sake of a good deal.

The Quest for Discounts

The culmination of Senior Discount Day often sees our intrepid seniors embarking on a treasure hunt through the mall, armed with flyers, coupons, and a shared determination to unearth the best deals. While aimed at savings, this pursuit inadvertently fosters a sense of camaraderie and collective joy among participants. Laughter echoes through the halls as they compare finds, share tips, and occasionally lead one another astray in a playful dance of misdirection. This quest, though chaotic, is a vibrant display of community, an illustration of how shared goals and communal experiences can weave individuals into a tapestry of mutual support and collective amusement.

Through these misadventures, from unexpected bargains to the humorous trials of technology, seniors navigate the landscape of discounts with a blend of wisdom, humor, and an unyielding zest for life. Each outing, whether it ends in laughter over miniature meals or shared tales of digital foibles, underscores the vibrancy of senior living. These experiences, rich in humor and warmth, are not merely about securing a bargain but about the stories crafted along the way, tales that weave into the larger narrative of life's joyful journey.

THE GREAT HEARING AID CONSPIRACY

In the heart of a close-knit community, a humorous theory took root among friends, suggesting their hearing aids were subjects of remote control antics. It began subtly, with one noticing his device's volume dipping during a riveting debate on the best pie recipes. Another recounted a tale where, amidst a family gathering, her hearing aid seemed to 'choose' to amplify the sound of clinking dishes over her grandchildren's laughter. This curious coincidence sparked playful speculation, evolving into a shared jest about a grand conspiracy aimed at the senior community, orchestrated by unseen forces with the power to control their auditory experiences.

This playful paranoia found its way into daily interactions, birthing a game of selective hearing. At gatherings, one might pretend their hearing aid had conveniently malfunctioned to sidestep an unwelcome inquiry about their garden's overzealous gnome population. Another would feign a sudden increase in volume to escape the endless retelling of a neighbor's fishing adventure. While rooted in jest, this game shed light on the intricate dance of communication among friends, where silence and sound became tools of wit and humor, weaving a complex tapestry of spoken and unspoken dialogue.

At one memorable party, this delicate balance met its match in a comedy of errors. The host, aware of his guests' penchant for selective hearing, decided to test their attentiveness with a game requiring precise listening. Instructions for a scavenger hunt whispered through the room, and it became a game of telephone gone awry. What started as a quest for "a book with a blue cover" somehow morphed into "look for the new lover," sending guests on a bemused search for romance rather than literature. The laughter that followed echoing through halls adorned with misplaced affection and confused participants, became a testament to the joy found in miscommunication, a reminder that even in misunderstanding, there is a chance for shared delight.

The culmination of these auditory adventures unfolded at a formal event, where the group, now seasoned in the art of hearing aid manipulation, decided to stage their technological triumph. With a twinkle of mischief, they coordinated a moment during the speeches where, on cue, all would adjust their hearing aids to emit a synchronized, high-pitched tone. The sound, barely audible to those outside their conspiratorial circle, was enough to halt the proceedings and send the group into fits of suppressed laughter. This act, a playful nod to their ongoing jest about remote-controlled devices, served as a gentle rebellion against the frustrations of aging, a declaration that joy and humor would not be muted by the passage of time or the whims of technology.

A deeper narrative unfolded through these episodes of mysterious malfunctions, selective hearing, and communication chaos. It was a narrative not of isolation but of connection, not of frustration but of laughter. In every misheard word, every deliberate adjustment, there lay an unspoken agreement among friends to face the vagaries of aging with a smile. For in the end, it was not the clarity of sound that mattered most, but the resonance of shared laughter, echoing through the years, a reminder that life, in all its unpredictability, was meant to be heard in all its vibrant, chaotic beauty.

THE QUEST FOR THE LOST GLASSES

Misplacing glasses is a universally understood dilemma, yet its occurrence among seniors transforms into a saga of frustration and unintended comedy. It begins innocently, with a momentary lapse of memory, a simple question - "Where did I leave my glasses?" - that spirals into an extensive search operation, turning homes upside down in a quest reminiscent of ancient treasure hunts. This search is not solitary; it enlists a cast of characters, each adding a layer of complexity and humor to the unfolding drama.

Pets, those loyal companions in life's journey, become unwitting allies in this quest. A dog's sudden interest in a previously ignored corner or a cat's fixation on what seems to be thin air often leads to corners and crannies unexplored by human eyes. While adding to the chaos, these moments weave a layer of warmth into the search, highlighting the silent bonds shared with our non-human friends. In these interactions, frustration gives way to laughter, a gentle reminder of the unexpected joys hidden in daily trials.

Grandchildren, with their boundless energy and curiosity, dive into the search with the enthusiasm of explorers discovering new lands. Their perspective, unclouded by the conventions of where things 'should' be, often leads to the most unexpected of places being investigated, from the refrigerator's crisper drawer to the cozy confines of a shoe. Their involvement turns the search into an adventure, a game that, while centered on the quest for the lost glasses, becomes a journey of discovery, of seeing the world through the unfiltered lens of youth and imagination.

In the face of repeated misplacements, inventive yet impractical solutions emerge, concocted from the depths of frustration and a desire to never again utter the phrase, "Have you seen my glasses?" Strings long enough to encircle a room are attached to frames, ensuring that while the glasses may still be misplaced, they are always within reach. Technology, too, is enlisted in this battle against forgetfulness, with gadgets designed to beep at the press of a button, leading one on an auditory treasure hunt that often ends in the realization that the glasses were atop one's head all along.

Yet, the true essence of this quest is unveiled in the revelation, the moment of finding. Glasses, those elusive spectacles without which the world remains a blur, are often found in the most obvious yet overlooked places. Resting on a bookshelf between novels that speak of adventures and lives lived fully or lying on a windowsill where they were absentmindedly set down to better appreciate the sunset, their discovery brings a flood of relief and an ironic chuckle. This moment, this simple yet profound finding serves as a mirror reflecting the larger picture of aging.

In the search for the lost glasses, a deeper narrative speaks to the heart of the human experience. It's a narrative woven from threads of memory, of moments lived and cherished, of the inevitable forgetfulness that comes with the passing of years, and of the laughter that echoes through it all. It's a reminder that, in the grand scheme of life, these small trials, these quests within the confines of our daily lives, color our days with the hues of frustration, joy, and unexpected discovery.

While seemingly trivial, the quest for the lost glasses encapsulates the essence of aging - a journey marked by mundane and profound challenges that are navigated with resilience, creativity, and a sense of humor. It underscores the importance of the connections that sustain us, be they with pets who offer silent companionship, grandchildren who remind us of the world's wonders, or friends who share in our frustrations and triumphs. And, perhaps most importantly, it serves as a gentle nudge, a reminder to embrace the intricacies of life with a smile, to find humor in our forgetfulness, and to celebrate the small victories, for in them lies the true beauty of growing older.

About - Padma Lakshmi. https://padmalakshmi.substack.com/about

CHAPTER 2

BRIDGING WORLDS WITH WORDS

In the kaleidoscope of life, the intergenerational exchange of words is akin to a dance—sometimes graceful, often clumsy, but always meaningful. Imagine standing on the edge of a canyon, shouting across the divide. The words you send across might not land in the way you expect. Sometimes, they echo back, distorted and unrecognizable. This is the challenge and charm of navigating the linguistic landscape that separates generations. It's not about the distances; it's about learning to tune into the frequencies that resonate with each other.

2.1 DECODING TEENAGE SLANG: A GRANDPARENT'S GUIDE

Language Lessons

Imagine a scenario that unfolds in many households, where the air is thick with the anticipation of families coming together. The stage is set for a grandparent attempting to connect with their teenage grandchild, armed with a freshly downloaded list of current slang terms. The mission: to speak their language. The result? A series of endearing misfires where "lit" describes the room's brightness, and "salty" is confused with the flavor of dinner. It's a scene that unfolds with the comedic timing of a sitcom, where the punchline is the laughter shared over the linguistic gap.

Cultural Exchange

Picture a Sunday afternoon, the air filled with the aroma of a family meal. Here, the exchange of words is not just a means of communication but a bridge across time. In a moment of jest, a grandparent decides to sprinkle their conversation with slang from their youth. Words like "groovy" and "bee's knees" float across the table, leaving the younger family members bemused. This prompts a trade-off, where each side teaches the other phrases from their time, turning the meal into an impromptu history lesson wrapped in humor and affection. It's a reminder that while words may change, the joy of sharing them is timeless.

Misinterpretations

A family gathers for a birthday celebration on a summer evening, the air alive with chatter and laughter. Amid the festivities, a grandparent employs some new slang to compliment their grandchild's outfit, aiming for "on fleek." Instead, "on the fleet" comes out, leading to a puzzled pause before the grandchild dissolves into giggles. The moment becomes a family anecdote, retold with relish, a testament to the endearing nature of miscommunication and the bonds it strengthens.

Bridge Building

In the tapestry of family life, words are the threads that bind. Consider a holiday gathering where exchanging stories and experiences across generations is a cherished ritual. Here, the attempt to bridge the linguistic divide becomes a collective endeavor. A game is proposed where each person shares a slang term from their generation, explaining its origins and usage. The room buzzes with excitement as phrases from decades past are juxtaposed with the vernacular of the internet age. It's a shared journey through the lexicon of life, where understanding blooms not from the perfection of communication but from the willingness to laugh, listen, and learn together.

This dance of words and meanings, of trial and error, is a testament to the enduring human desire to connect, understand, and belong. It underscores the power of language not just as a tool for communication but as a vessel for history, culture, and affection. In the laughter shared over linguistic mishaps, in the warmth that spreads through a room when understanding dawns, we find the true essence of family—a connection that transcends words, reaching deep into the heart of what it means to love and be loved.

2.2 THE ANNUAL TECH SUPPORT VISIT: GRANDKIDS TO THE RESCUE

Anticipation thickens the air in homes across the globe, not for the holiday seasons you might expect, but for a visit now humorously enshrined in family lore as the "annual tech support visit." It's that particular time of year when the younger generation descends upon their grandparents' abode, armed with the patience of saints and the tech-savvy Silicon Valley prodigies. The air buzzes with the promise of digital enlightenment, a period marked by the eager, if not slightly anxious, faces of seniors awaiting the mysteries of the modern world to be unraveled by their kin.

The initiation of these tech tutorials is often as unpredictable as it is fraught with comedic potential. Picture a scene where a grandparent is presented with a new tablet, a device heralded for its ability to connect, entertain, and simplify. Yet, what unfolds is a series of taps, swipes, and presses that lead not to enlightenment but to the accidental purchase of a year's supply of dog food, a subscription to a Mongolian throat singing channel, and the mysterious disappearance of all app icons from the home screen. In these moments of bewilderment and unintended digital chaos, laughter becomes the bridge over the generational tech divide, a shared joy in the absurdity of misadventure.

Yet, the dance of digits and screens is only sometimes led by the young. Enter the realm of outdated technology, where VCRs still blink at 12:00, and flip phones are not ironic accessories but trusted tools. Here, a grandchild's encounter with such artifacts becomes a journey into the archives of technological history. In the tech years, they have held ancient relics and devices, leading to a reversal of roles. The grandparent becomes the sage, explaining the art of programming a VCR to record a beloved weekly show or the skill required to text on a numeric keypad. This exchange, rich in its reversal, highlights not just the rapid pace of technological evolution but the enduring nature of curiosity and the joy found in discovery, regardless of the direction in which it flows.

As the visit progresses, small victories are celebrated with the enthusiasm of moon landings. A grandparent learns to video call, their face alight with the magic of seeing a loved one's smile cross continents in real-time. Yet, in this triumph, there lies a twist. The first call is made not to a family member but to the bewildered pizza delivery service, resulting in a confused but humorous exchange with a delivery driver now face-to-face with a senior marveling at the miracle of technology. Such moments, where success is tinged with the unexpected, serve as gentle reminders of the beauty of learning in merging human intent with the whims of technology.

These visits, marked by laughter, frustration, and the occasional unplanned pizza order, are about more than troubleshooting or updating software. They are rituals of connection, moments where the baton of knowledge is passed back and forth between generations, each teaching the other in a cycle as continuous as it is precious. There lies a story through every locked screen, accidental app deletion, and successful video chat. It's a narrative that weaves through the laughter and challenges, a tapestry rich with the threads of shared experiences, a reminder that in every confused click and triumphant text, the true triumph is in the togetherness, in the shared journey through the ever-evolving landscape of technology.

2.3 THE THANKSGIVING TURKEY THAT ALMOST FLEW AWAY

The annual preparation of the Thanksgiving turkey, an endeavor steeped in tradition and anticipation, unfailingly metamorphoses into an epic tale of culinary ambition marred by slapstick calamities. On this particular morning, the kitchen transforms into a stage for a comedy of errors, where the turkey, the feast's centerpiece, becomes an unwilling protagonist in a sequence of mishaps. A slip of the hand sends spices flying in a colorful cloud, a misjudged oven door swing results in an impromptu game of hot potato with the bird, and an ill-timed sneeze launches a flurry of feathers back onto the plucked masterpiece. Each incident, while a setback in the culinary process, adds layers to the day's lore, weaving a story that will garnish the family's tales for generations.

As the day unfolds, a cast of unexpected allies emerges, drawn by the commotion and the irresistible aroma of cooking that wafts beyond the confines of the kitchen. Neighbors, lured by the promise of shared laughter (and perhaps a slice of pie), lend their hands and anecdotes to the proceedings. Each brings their spice, be it a secret ingredient or a tale of Thanksgiving misadventures from their archives. Pets, too, find themselves embroiled in the day's events, from the dog appointed as the turkey's guardian (a role it interprets as an invitation to a staring contest) to the cat that decides the kitchen counter is the prime location for a nap amidst the chaos. Their antics, though occasionally adding to the pandemonium, weave a sense of unity and shared endeavor into the fabric of the day.

In an unexpected twist, the turkey decides to stage its dramatic rebellion. A precarious placement, a nudge too far, and suddenly, the bird is on the move, sliding across the counter in a bid for freedom that culminates in a spectacular dive onto the floor. What follows is a scene that would not be out of place in a slapstick comedy—a wild chase ensues, with family members, neighbors, and pets forming a spontaneous and chaotic al-

107 SHORT HUMOROUS LIFE STORIES FOR SE...   39

liance in pursuit of the wayward feast. Laughter peals louder than the calls for the turkey to halt its escape, turning the quest into a spectacle that rivals the main event for entertainment.

Finally, as the sun begins to dip below the horizon, casting long shadows and bathing the kitchen in a warm, forgiving light, the turkey, a little worse for wear but triumphantly retrieved, finds its place at the center of the table. The family, joined by their impromptu guests, gathers around, their laughter mingling with the flickering candlelight. The day's events, from the initial mishaps to the turkey's ill-fated escape attempt, are recounted with glee, each retelling adding embellishments and eliciting fresh peals of laughter. It is in this moment, surrounded by the warmth of shared stories and the glow of togetherness, that the essence of Thanksgiving reveals itself—not in the perfection of the feast but in the joy of the shared experience, in the laughter that binds and in the stories that will be carried forward, a testament to the day when the turkey almost flew away.

In the end, these shared moments, filled with laughter and the warmth of togetherness, etch themselves into our memories, painting a picture of life that's vibrant, chaotic, and utterly beautiful. The mishaps and mayhem, the unexpected allies, and the great escape all weave into a narrative richer for its imperfections, a story shared across generations, binding us in a common thread of joy and resilience. It's a reminder that, in the grand tapestry of life, the shared laughter and love genuinely make us rich. As we turn the page from this chapter, we carry forward the light-hearted spirit, ready to embrace the next adventure with open hearts and a readiness to find joy in the unexpected.

I Hope You Enjoyed a Good Laugh!

Thank you for choosing "107 Short Humorous Life Stories for Seniors"! I hope that each story brought you not only a smile but also kindled delightful memories and conversations.

Your feedback is incredibly important to me and to other readers who are considering this book. I would be grateful if you could take a few minutes to share your thoughts on Amazon. Your review could help others decide whether this book is right for them!

How to Leave a Review:

1. Visit the product page on Amazon.
2. Scroll down to the "Customer Reviews" section.
3. Click on "Write a customer review."
4. Rate the book and write your thoughts.

Alternatively, you can use your smartphone to scan the QR code below to be taken directly to the review page:

Or, if you prefer, click on the following link:

https://amzn.to/3V6U776

Thank you for your time and for helping us and your fellow readers. We look forward to hearing your thoughts!

CHAPTER 3

THE UNSCRIPTED SYMPHONY OF RETIREMENT

In the golden era of retirement, every day unfurls like an unscripted symphony, where the unexpected becomes the main melody, crafting a series of events as unpredictable as they are enriching. It's a time when the map of life gets redrawn, not with the precision of GPS, but through the serendipitous detours and mishaps that chart a course to laughter and newfound wisdom. This chapter delves into one such adventure—a road trip that veers off the beaten path, transforming a routine journey into an odyssey of discovery, mishaps, and, ultimately, a celebration of the spontaneity that retirement affords.

3.1 THE RV ROAD TRIP MISHAP

Route Confusion

Imagine a scenario where a couple, newly embraced by the freedom of retirement, decides to take their gleaming RV on its maiden voyage across the scenic byways. They set off with maps that have seen better days and a sense of adventure that far outweighs their navigational skills. The roadmap, however, more a relic of road trips past than a reliable guide, soon leads them astray. Refusal to ask for directions becomes a testament to their independence, turning their journey into a comical odyssey. It's akin to assembling furniture without instructions: a blend of overconfidence and improvisation that, despite frustrations, often results in unexpected satisfaction and a story worth recounting.

Campsite Comedy

Their arrival at the campsite, intended as a triumphant commencement of their outdoor sojourn, unfolds with the grace of a sitcom scene. The RV, a behemoth in their untrained hands, becomes a prop in a slapstick performance of errors. Neighbors, drawn by the commotion—or perhaps the promise of entertainment—offer unsolicited advice and assistance. The couple's attempts at setting up, marked by a battle with a seemingly sentient awning and a series of misplaced stakes, highlight an often-overlooked truth: the process, with all its trials and errors, is as much a part of the adventure as the destination itself.

The Detour Adventure

Motivated by a stubborn reliance on their outdated map, a wrong turn steers them into the heart of an unplanned detour. What at first seems a misstep soon reveals itself as the heart of their adventure. They stumble upon a small town, its charm unmarked on any tourist map, where they're greeted not just by the sights but by the souls that define it. A local festival, stumbled upon by chance, offers them a taste of community and celebration that no travel brochure could encapsulate. Friendships form, stories are exchanged, and the realization dawns that the best discoveries are those not sought but serendipitously found.

Homecoming

Upon their return, the RV, now less a vehicle and more a vessel of their memories, carry the dust of roads less traveled, and the echoes of laughter shared. The mishaps that once seemed like hurdles now form the highlights of their tales. They return not just souvenirs but with stories, the currency of experience. Their odyssey, with its detours and misadventures, enriches their retirement, not by ticking off destinations but by weaving a tapestry of moments that celebrate the joy of the unexpected. It's a reaffirmation that in retirement, as in life, the journey itself is the destination, rich with the potential for discovery, growth, and laughter.

In the retirement narrative, each day offers a blank page on which to script new adventures and chart courses unbounded by time constraints or convention expectations. The road trip, with its mishaps and misdirections, serves as a microcosm of this more extensive journey, a reminder that unexpected detours often lead to the most memorable destinations. Through the lens of these experiences, retirement reveals itself not as a period of winding down but as a stage for exploration, for embracing the spontaneity and unpredictability that give life its flavor and joy.

3.2 THE GOLF CART CHASE AT SUNRISE VILLAGE

In the heart of Sunrise Village, a retirement community where the pace of life meanders as leisurely as the river nearby, an event unfolded that would ripple through its tranquil routine like a stone skipping over still water. It began with an innocuous challenge, a jest between neighbors over whose golf cart could navigate the village's winding paths with more grace and speed. This light-hearted competition sparked over morning coffee, and laughter soon burgeoned into an event that would etch itself into the community's collective memory.

Friendly Rivalry

Though rooted in jest, the rivalry carried an undercurrent of the competitive spirit that age had not dimmed but merely refined. Each participant, dressed in attire that was as much a statement of their personality as practical for the race, lined up at the agreed starting point. The air buzzed with a mix of anticipation and the electric whir of golf carts at the ready. Onlookers, having chosen their champions, offered last-minute advice and adjustments, their banter adding to the atmosphere of camaraderie that enveloped the event. As the signal to start was given, a cheer erupted, sending the carts off in a display of speed that was more about flair than velocity, a parade of determination and glee.

Community Cheerleaders

Soon, the entirety of Sunrise Village found itself drawn into the spectacle. Previously content with their morning routines, residents emerged as an impromptu audience, lining the route with chairs and makeshift banners. The event, transforming into a village-wide affair, saw allegiances formed over shared histories and friendships, each cheerleader donning the colors of their chosen racer. Laughter filled the air, punctuated by the occasional good-natured heckle, as the community, for a moment, set aside the tranquility of their days for the thrill of the chase. This unity, born of shared amusement and spirited competition, highlighted the vibrant social tapestry that wove the residents together, a reminder that life within the village was as much about the bonds formed in moments of joy as it was about the peaceful days that preceded and would follow.

Unexpected Obstacles

The course was challenging, meandering through the village like a slow-moving stream. Once admired for their beauty, garden decorations now served as hurdles to be navigated with a mix of skill and humor. A flock of geese, residents as much as any human within the village, chose this day to assert their dominion over the paths, their procession across the route a stately interruption that drew laughter and applause. Each obstacle, whether animate or inanimate, added a layer to the story being written that day, a testament to the unpredictable nature of life and the joy found in its navigation. These interruptions, far from detracting from the event, enriched it, offering opportunities for displays of quick thinking and hearty laughter from the unexpected.

The Finish Line

As the race drew to a close, with the finish line in sight and the community gathered in a crescent of anticipation, it became evident that the outcome mattered less than the journey. The racers, approaching the end, slowed, their competitive fervor giving way to an understanding that the true victory lay in the shared experience, the laughter, and the stories that would emerge from this day. The finish line, crossed in a group rather than in sequence, became a symbol not of individual triumph but of communal celebration. The following gathering, marked by tales of the race, shared meals, and contentedness from a well-spent day, underscored the essence of life at Sunrise Village. It was a reminder that, within this community, every day held the potential for adventure, for moments that, though unplanned, would become cherished memories, threads in the rich tapestry of their collective experience.

In this way, the golf cart chase at Sunrise Village transcended its beginnings as a simple competition, evolving into a celebration of life, laughter, and the enduring spirit of community. It stood as a testament to the fact that, regardless of age, the desire for connection, for moments of unbridled joy and shared endeavor, remains a constant. This beacon guides the human experience toward its most luminous expressions.

3.3 GARDENING WARS: THE BATTLE OF THE NEIGHBORS

In the quietude of a neighborhood where the most excitement usually stemmed from the weekly farmers' market, an unforeseen rivalry took root, quite literally, between two households. It began as a benign contest of blooms, a challenge thrown down during a casual over-the-fence chat about whose rose bushes held the most promise. However, what unfolded was a saga that transformed the tranquil lanes into arenas of horticultural ambition, where flowers and foliage became the unlikely soldiers in a duel of gardening prowess.

Competitive Planting

The opening salvo was innocuous—a meticulously arranged bed of tulips, their vibrant heads nodding gently in the spring breeze. Yet, this floral display soon beckoned a response in the form of an elaborate labyrinth of lavender, its aroma wafting through the neighborhood, enticing not just bees but the curious glances of passersby. Each subsequent addition to the gardens escalated in complexity and splendor, from cascading water features to exotic specimens that whispered of distant lands. Once humble refuges of relaxation, the gardens morphed into canvases of competitive spirit, a testament to the lengths to which the neighbors would go to claim the title of the street's supreme gardener.

Espionage and Strategy

As the competition intensified, so too did the tactics employed. The cover of night bore witness to secretive sorties across lawns, with each party armed with flashlights and seed packets, engaging in clandestine plantings to surprise and outdo the other. Daylight revealed the results of these nocturnal missions—a sudden eruption of sunflowers here, a stealthily introduced patch of wildflowers there, each addition a move in a chess game played with greenery. Strategies evolved, from the deliberate positioning of bird feeders to attract avian allies in seed dispersal to the installation of artfully concealed irrigation systems designed to nurture their botanical charges to perfection.

Unexpected Consequences

Yet, as the gardens burgeoned and bloomed with the fruits of this rivalry, they began to attract more than just competitive glances. Wildlife, drawn by the abundance and variety, turned the neighborhood into a bustling ecosystem where birds, bees, and even the occasional deer found sanctuary. Furthermore, the wider community noticed the spectacle of the dueling gardens. What began as a local curiosity soon blossomed into a minor tourist attraction, with visitors meandering through the lanes, cameras in hand, capturing the floral fantasia that had unfolded. This influx of admirers brought a measure of fame to the neighborhood and a sense of pride in the unexpected beauty that had been cultivated from rivalry.

Truce and Triumph

As summer waned into the mellow warmth of autumn, the fervor of competition gradually gave way to a reflection on the journey that had transpired. The realization dawned that they had inadvertently gifted each other and their community with a spectacle of nature's splendor in their quest for supremacy. The decision to declare a truce was marked not by a ceremonial handshake but by planning a joint garden party. This celebration would unite the neighborhood in the spaces that sparked the rivalry. As the sun dipped below the horizon, bathing the gardens in golden light, laughter, and music filled the air, mingling with the scents of blooms that had been the cause of so much contention but now stood as symbols of unity and shared accomplishment. In this moment of communal joy, the battle of the neighbors culminated not in the victory of one but in a triumph for all, a testament to the transformative power of passion, however competitively it might begin.

Ultimately, the tapestry of life, with its myriad hues and textures, is often woven from threads of the most unexpected colors. The saga of the gardening wars, while rooted in rivalry, blossomed into a narrative of community, creativity, and the shared human impulse to bring beauty into the world. As we turn our gaze from the gardens back to the broader landscape of our lives, we carry with us the reminder that from the seeds of competition, we can grow the most unexpected and enriching harvests.

Let us step lightly into the next chapter, where the canvas broadens, the palette shifts and new stories await to be sown and nurtured in the garden of our collective journey.

CHAPTER 4

ECHOES OF LAUGHTER: A NOSTALGIC TRIP THROUGH TIME

In a corner of memory where the past mingles with the echoes of laughter, the tales of yesteryears await, eager to leap off the pages and into the hearts of those who dare to reminisce. Here, within the faded photographs of our minds, the vibrant beats of the 70s disco era still pulse with life, inviting us to step back onto the dance floor of memories, if only for a moment. In these recollections, the essence of joy, resilience, and the unbridled spirit of an era come alive, painting our past with the glittering hues of disco balls and bell-bottoms.

4.1 THE DISCO BALL DISASTER: A 70S FIASCO

A Night to Remember

The anticipation was palpable, thick as the summer humidity, as the community hall transformed into a time capsule for the night. Streamers in psychedelic hues crisscrossed the ceiling, flares of color against the dim, anticipation-filled room. A disco ball hung at the center of it all, suspended like the moon in a starless sky, its mirrored surface winking mischievously at the assembled crowd below. The air was electric, charged with the promise of nostalgia, as tracks from decades past waited in the wings, ready to transport the gathering to an era where the music never died, and the dance floor was sacred ground.

Unexpected Spin

No sooner had the first notes of a classic hit shimmied through the speakers than the disco ball, that emblem of 70s revelry, decided to take on a life of its own. A faulty wire, perhaps, or the universe conspiring to add its twist to the tale, sent it spinning in a dizzying dance far beyond its intended waltz. It whirled like a planet off its axis, casting scattered beams of light that turned the dance floor into a kaleidoscope. Laughter erupted as dancers, momentarily caught in a whirlwind of light, found partners in a farce they hadn't rehearsed. The chaotic scene held the room in the grip of joy, a collective embrace of the unexpected turn the night had taken.

Groovy Recovery

The community, a tapestry woven from threads of shared histories and laughter, rallied with the resilience of a troupe unfazed by stage mishaps. A ladder, procured as if by magic, and a volunteer, braver than most, emerged from the ranks. A precarious ascent, under the watchful eyes of the disco's denizens, aimed to corral the rogue sphere. Below, the crowd, undeterred, swayed, and twisted, their movements a homage to an era that celebrated the spontaneous, the unplanned. Now subdued and spinning at a sedate pace, the disco ball resumed its role as the night's beacon, a nod to the collective effort that had averted disaster. The incident, far from dampening spirits, served to amplify the sense of camaraderie, a shared victory against the odds.

Lessons Learned

As the last notes faded and the lights brightened, reflections on the evening's escapade took a poignant turn in the aftermath. The disco ball disaster, now etched in the annals of community lore, stood as a testament to the enduring power of laughter and the strength found in unity. It reminded everyone of the days when disco ruled the airwaves, when challenges were met with a dance move, and resilience was as much a part of the wardrobe as polyester and platform shoes. The night, with its unexpected twist, underscored a universal truth, as relevant today as it was in the era of disco: that joy can be found amid chaos and that laughter is the melody that keeps the spirit dancing long after the music stops.

Visual Element: A Step Back in Time

A collage of vintage photos from the 70s disco era, interspersed with community hall event images, captured the night's essence and the spirit of recovery. The photos, annotated with humorous captions, invite the viewer to share in the collective memory and the joy that danced through the evening.

In this vivid tableau of images, the essence of the 70s and the spirit of the community come together, a visual symphony that celebrates not just an era but the timeless nature of joy, resilience, and the bonds that laughter forges. Through these snapshots, we're reminded that while the disco ball may have stopped spinning, the stories it inspired continue to resonate, echoes of laughter that linger in the corridors of our memories, inviting us to dance once more in the light of bygone days.

4.2 THE GREAT JELL-O SALAD INCIDENT OF '65

In an era when culinary adventures were as much about the spectacle as they were about sustenance, one ambitious soul set their sights on creating a Jell-O salad masterpiece for the upcoming community potluck. The vision was grand: a layered marvel, a cornucopia of fruits suspended in a prism of gelatin, each stratum a testament to the assembler's culinary acumen. This was to be no ordinary contribution to the communal table but a work of art. This gastronomic delight would leave onlookers in awe and palates in anticipation.

The undertaking began with a meticulous selection of ingredients, each chosen for its vibrant hue and the promise of adding flavor and visual drama to the dish. The kitchen transformed into a laboratory, with packets of gelatin in every rainbow color arrayed like paint on an artist's palette, ready to be combined into a culinary masterpiece. However, the line between ambition and overreach blurred as the assembly progressed. Adding too many elements, each vying for dominance, led to a kaleidoscopic aberration. Fruits meant to be delicately suspended in their respective layers melded into one another, their colors bleeding together to create shades not found in nature nor in any cook's guide. The result was a dish that defied categorization. This vibrant but bewildering spectacle bore little resemblance to the harmonious creation envisioned.

As the potluck approached, the creator of this jiggling jamboree faced a dilemma: to present their creation with pride or to retreat in the face of culinary misadventure. In a decision that epitomized the spirit of the times, they shared their experiment with the community, a bold move that turned the potluck into an unforgettable event. The unveiling of the Jell-O salad elicited reactions ranging from bemusement to glee. Rather than the critique and consternation they had braced for, the community responded with laughter and good-natured ribbing. Friends and neighbors gathered around the quivering gelatin mass. They offered their interpretations of the dish, each more outlandish than the last. Some saw in its swirling colors a psychedelic representation of the era. In contrast, others playfully debated whether it was more a dessert or a salad. This question defies resolution.

In the spirit of the potluck, where sharing and camaraderie were the authentic dishes of the day, the Jell-O salad became the centerpiece not of the table but of the conversation. Tales of culinary misfires from potlucks past were shared, each story adding to the tapestry of community lore. The incident became a catalyst for laughter, a reminder that the value of these gatherings lay not in the perfection of the dishes brought to the table but in the stories and memories created around them. In all its confounding glory, the Jell-O salad was passed around, each tentative taste followed by a chorus of chuckles and shared glances. Even those who dared not sample the creation found joy in the spectacle, the boldness of the attempt, and the openness with which it was shared.

As the evening waned and the potluck drew to a close, the Jell-O salad, now a legend in its own right, served as a poignant reminder of the beauty found in imperfection. It was not the flawlessly executed dishes that lingered in the minds of those present but the vibrant, inedible concoction that had brought them together in laughter and mutual appreciation. The incident underscored a truth often overlooked in the pursuit of culinary or any other form of perfection: the missteps and the unexpected detours that imbue our endeavors with character and our gatherings with warmth. The Great Jell-O Salad Incident of '65, while a culinary misadventure, became a cherished memory, a story to be passed down through generations, a testament to the joy that can be found in the shared acceptance of our fallibilities.

4.3 WHEN BELL BOTTOMS RULED THE WORLD

The era when bell bottoms weren't just attire but a declaration of identity, a rebellion stitched in denim and polyester, unfurls tales of sartorial audacity met with both admiration and gentle mockery. Those were days when the flare from knee to heel wasn't merely about fashion but a symbol of liberation, a canvas upon which the era's youth painted their hopes, dreams, and the vibrant colors of their individuality. In recalling these times, one can't help but chuckle over the earnestness with which these flared treasures were donned, the careful selection of patterns that could either set one at the pinnacle of style or, just as likely, tip them into the realm of the fashion faux pas.

Within this flamboyant tableau, a high-stakes dance competition loomed an event where the prowess on the dance floor was as much about the moves as it was about the magnificence of one's bell bottoms. Participants glided, twisted, and spun, their flares creating mesmerizing visuals, a spectacle of fabric and motion enthralling onlookers. Yet, these same prized trousers proved a challenge as ambitious moves met with excess fabric, leading to humorous entanglements that only added to the spectacle. Despite these hiccups, the competition displayed camaraderie, where the occasional stumble or misstep was met with laughter and applause, a celebration of effort over perfection.

As outlandish as it might have appeared to onlookers from other generations, this trend fostered a sense of unity among its adherents. Bell bottoms became more than just clothing; they were the banner under which the youth of the time rallied, a symbol that marked gatherings, be they at dance halls or the more spontaneous congregations at parks and street corners. These were not merely meetups but events where music blared from boomboxes, stories were shared, and friendships were forged, all under the watchful gaze of those iconic trousers. It was a time when style served as a bridge, connecting individuals through shared tastes and mutual appreciation for the boldness of their era's fashion.

Reflecting upon these trends from the present vantage point, one can't help but marvel at the cyclical nature of fashion, the way styles once derided as outlandish find their way back into the spotlight, celebrated and embraced by a new generation. This retrospective amusement isn't tinged with regret but with a fondness for the joy found in embracing the trends of the times, no matter how fleeting or silly they may seem in retrospect. It serves as a reminder that fashion, in all its forms, is an expression of the zeitgeist, a reflection of the collective mood, aspirations, and, at times, the rebellious spirit of the age.

From bell bottoms to the myriad of trends that have since taken their place, each wave of fashion brings stories of individuality, shared moments, and the continuous thread of human creativity that weaves through the fabric of time. These recollections stand not as mere nostalgia but as chapters in the larger narrative of our shared history, a testament to the enduring power of self-expression and the bonds it fosters among those who dare to wear their identity for the world to see.

As we close this chapter on the whimsical whirlwind of bell bottoms and the era they epitomized, we carry forward the laughter, the shared memories, and the reminder that in every stitch of our varied attire, there lies a story waiting to be told. The flares of the past remind us of the richness of our collective journey, a tapestry of trends that, in their time, were the markers of identity, rebellion, and unity.

In the dance of life, where the music changes but the floor remains, we move to the rhythm of our era, clothed in the trends that speak to us, always forward, always together, always with a touch of the joy that fashion, in its essence, brings to our lives.

CHAPTER 5

THE ECHOES OF
SIMPLE ACTS

I n the panorama of life's experiences, the tiniest pebbles often create the most enduring ripples. A penny, the smallest denomination of currency, holds within its copper clasp not just economic value but the potential to craft narratives of generosity, kindness, and communal spirit far surpassing its monetary worth. This chapter unfolds the tale of a simple penny jar, an emblem of thrift that transforms into a beacon of community strength and individual growth, illustrating the profound impact of seemingly inconsequential acts.

5.1 THE PENNY JAR: A LESSON IN SAVING

Simple Beginnings

In a modest kitchen, sunlight streams through the window, casting a warm glow on a glass jar perched on the counter. Its contents, a collection of pennies, shimmer like tiny beacons of possibility. This jar, introduced to a young person by their guardian as a tool for learning the value of saving, begins its life as an empty vessel, waiting to be filled one penny at a time. Each coin, earned from chores or gifted during special occasions, drops into the jar with a satisfying clink. This sound marks not just the growth of savings but the planting of a seed, the understanding that even the most minor contributions can accumulate into something significant.

Unexpected Generosity

As the jar nears its brim, its purpose evolves. A neighbor, known to the family for their kindness yet currently facing hardship, becomes the unintended beneficiary of the penny jar's contents. This decision, made collectively one evening around the kitchen table, transforms the act of saving into one of giving. The jar, carried to the neighbor's door with both eager and hesitant hands, becomes a symbol of communal support, a small gesture carrying the weight of empathy and shared humanity. The neighbor's profound and heartfelt gratitude underscores a lesson far greater than the value of saving: the impact of generosity and how even the most modest acts of kindness can light up the darkest of times.

Community Effort

Word of this simple act of kindness ripples through the community, inspiring others to start their penny jars. Soon, windowsills and counter-tops across the neighborhood boast jars, each a testament to the power of collective action. This movement, sparked by the actions of one family, led to the formation of a fund dedicated to assisting those in need within the community. Meetings in living rooms and backyards become spaces where plans are hatched, and resources pooled, not just financially but in skills and time. The penny jar idea, now a community-wide initiative, fosters unexpected bonds among neighbors, turning acquaintances into allies with a common goal.

Lasting Impact

Reflecting on the journey of the penny jar, from its inception as a lesson in saving to its role in galvanizing a community, its true significance becomes clear. It serves as a reminder that lessons learned in the simplicity of childhood often carry the most profound wisdom. The habit of saving, instilled by the clinking of pennies in a jar, blossoms into a broader understanding of value, not measured in currency but in the richness of giving and the strength of community ties. This story, rooted in saving and sharing, echoes the timeless truth that minor actions can lead to the most meaningful outcomes.

Visual Element: The Ripple Effect Infographic

An infographic titled "The Ripple Effect of a Penny Jar" visually captures the journey of the penny jar from a personal saving tool to a community-wide effort of generosity. Through concentric circles, it illustrates how the act of saving, symbolized by a single penny, expands into larger circles of impact—supporting a neighbor, inspiring a community, and strengthening bonds. Each circle is annotated with critical moments and outcomes, providing a visual narrative of how small acts can generate significant waves of change.

Every penny saved and given lies a story of growth, compassion, and community. In its simplicity, the penny jar teaches us to look beyond the face value of our actions and see the potential for profound impact in even the most minor deeds. It reminds us that in the economy of kindness, every contribution counts, and every act of generosity enriches the recipient, the giver, and the wider community. Through the lens of the penny jar, we are invited to reevaluate our understanding of value to recognize that the true wealth of our lives is measured not in currency but in the moments of connection and acts of kindness that define our shared humanity.

5.2 THE LOST LETTER: RECONNECTING OLD FRIENDS

In the quiet of an afternoon, when the sun hung low, casting long shadows that danced upon the walls of a well-loved home, a letter, yellowed with age and sealed with intentions long forgotten, emerged from the depths of a neglected drawer. Its discovery, accidental amidst a search for something far less significant, halted time, wrapping the finder in a shroud of anticipation and trepidation. This envelope, addressed in the looping script characteristic of an era when penmanship held as much weight as the words themselves, bore the potential to bridge the chasm that years had eroded between two souls once inseparable.

The act of unfolding the letter, its creases re-sisting the intrusion like guards to a long-sealed tomb, was a pilgrimage back to days bathed in the golden hue of youth. The words, though faded, pulsed with life, each sentence a beacon illumi-nating memories that had dimmed in the relent-less march of time. There, in the neat rows of ink, lay recounted tales of mischief and milestones, of dreams painted with the broad strokes of naivety and ambition. The letter, a time capsule of shared experiences, evoked a cascade of emotions, from the laughter that bubbled up at the recollection of escapades best left unmentioned to the pang of nostalgia for moments that, once lived, had slipped quietly into the ether of the past.

The revelation that the long-thought-lost letter had simply been misplaced turned the wheels of fate, propelling its recipient on a quest for recon-nection and reconciliation with time. The deci-sion to seek out the friend who had, decades ago, poured their heart into words was not made lightly. It was a step into the unknown, a disrup-tion of the status quo that had, over the years, be-come a comfortable, if not entirely satisfying, existence. Yet, the potential to rekindle a bond that had once defined the essence of friendship outweighed the hesitance, setting the stage for a reunion that was as much about rediscovering the other as it was about finding oneself.

When it occurred, the meeting was less a dramatic climax than a gentle unfolding, a testament to the enduring nature of genuine connections. Time, it seemed, had not so much built walls as it had laid a blanket over the embers of their friendship, embers that now, gently coaxed back to life, glowed with the warmth of familiarity and affection. The exchange was not marked by grand gestures but by sharing life's minutiae, the years in between bridged by stories of triumphs and trials, laughter and loss. The acknowledgment of paths diverged and lives lived apart gave way to the realization that the core of their bond, the shared values, and mutual respect, remained untarnished by time.

This rekindling, sparked by a forgotten letter, illuminated the truth that friendships, even those interrupted by life's vicissitudes, carry within them the resilience to withstand the erosion of time. Once a vessel of thoughts and emotions, the letter transformed into a beacon that guided two individuals back to a shared harbor, a safe haven where the passage of time was rendered insignificant against the backdrop of a reawakened camaraderie.

In the quiet aftermath of their reunion, as the initial euphoria gave way to a contemplative calm, the power of the written word revealed itself in its entire splendor. The letter, a simple composition of ink and paper, had transcended its physical form to become a catalyst for healing and growth, a reminder of the impact our words can have on the lives of others. It underscored the importance of reaching out, bridging the silences that life often imposes, with the simple yet profound act of sharing our thoughts, fears, and joys. The realization dawned that in this age of instantaneous communication, where words are often dispensed with the rapidity and thoughtlessness of keystrokes, the deliberate act of writing, of imprinting one's essence onto paper, holds an intimacy and significance that transcends the ephemeral nature of digital exchanges.

The reunion, facilitated by the discovery of a lost letter, served as a reconnection between friends and a reflection on the essence of human interaction. It was a vivid illustration of the enduring impact of our words, a call to embrace the vulnerability that comes with expressing our thoughts, and an encouragement to reach out to those who have imprinted themselves on our lives. In the quiet moments that followed their meeting, as the sun dipped below the horizon, casting the day into the soft embrace of twilight, the significance of their journey from estrangement back to friendship settled around them like a cloak woven from threads of gratitude, understanding, and an appreciation for the serendipitous twists of fate that, sometimes, lead us back to where we belong.

5.3 THE HOMEMADE SOAP BOX DERBY

In the heart of a community where the rhythm of daily life hums with a quiet consistency, an initiative sparked a collective endeavor that would soon become a cherished annual tradition—the creation of a homemade soap box derby. This event, conceived from the dual desires to foster creativity and tighten the bonds among neighbors, transformed empty lots and silent streets into arenas of imagination and camaraderie. Families, friends, and solo artisans alike set about constructing their soap box cars, each vehicle a reflection of its creators' unique stories and dreams. Garages and driveways became makeshift workshops. Old crates and discarded wheels were reborn as chariots of whimsy and speed, adorned with paint, decals, and the occasional improbable spoiler fashioned from household detritus.

The crescendo of anticipation peaked as the derby day dawned, a spectacle of community spirit and friendly rivalry under the benevolent gaze of a sun that seemed to approve of the proceedings. The air, crisp and expectant, vibrated with the crowd's buzz and the participants' nervous excitement. Laughter punctuated the atmosphere, a melody that danced around the palpable sense of unity enveloping the event. As the flag waved to signal the start, a motley parade of soap box cars, each a testament to the creativity and ingenuity of its builders, hurtled down the makeshift track. Cheers and encouragement cascaded from the sidelines, a torrent of support that fueled the racers as much as the thrill of the descent.

Within this chaos of motion and emotion, the race unfolded with twists that none could have predicted. Cars that seemed destined for victory based on their sleek designs wobbled and veered. At the same time, the underdogs, those constructed with more heart than aerodynamics in mind, navigated the course with a surprising grace. Rather than being a place of fierce contention, the finish line became a scene of jubilation for all, regardless of the order crossed. In this derby, the true victors were not those who reached the end first but those who embodied the spirit of endeavor and innovation. Awards were distributed not for speed but for creativity, for the audacity to dream and build outside the confines of conventional design. It was a celebration not of competition but of the shared joy in creation and participation.

Amidst the scattered tools and the remnants of construction, the lessons of the derby began to crystallize. This event, more than a race, was a lesson in collaboration, where the exchange of ideas and assistance between teams underscored the value of working together towards a common goal. It highlighted the importance of creativity, not merely as an exercise in aesthetics but as a way of thinking, a means to approach problems and challenges with an open mind and a willingness to experiment. Moreover, it celebrated the sheer joy of taking part, of being a component of something larger than oneself, where the outcome, while delightful, paled in comparison to the experience of the journey.

As the day waned and the crowds dispersed, leaving behind trails of laughter and footprints of joy, the essence of the derby lingered. It was a testament to the capacity of simple, heartfelt endeavors to weave individuals into a tighter community fabric, to transform ordinary streets into canvases of collective expression, and to turn neighbors into collaborators and friends. In the wake of the derby, the community stood a little closer, bound by the shared memories of a day when cars built of dreams and determination raced not for glory but for the pure delight of the endeavor.

In this reflection on the homemade soap box derby, the narratives of cooperation, creativity, and the intrinsic value of participation emerge as the guiding themes. These stories, woven from the fabric of a community coming together to build, race, and celebrate, remind us of the profound impact of communal activities on the social tapestry of our lives. They highlight the beauty of collective creativity, the strength found in mutual support, and the joy inherent in shared experiences. As we turn the page from this chapter, we carry with us the lessons of the derby—a reminder of the power of community, the importance of creativity, and the value of wholeheartedly joining in the dance of life's unscripted symphony.

CHAPTER 6

WHEN HISTORY BECKONED, WE ANSWERED WITH JOY

In the tapestry of human experience, specific threads shimmer with the collective anticipation of momentous occasions—events that beckon us to gather, to share in the wonder and the promise of progress. The moon landing, that monumental leap for mankind, was one such thread, weaving together the hopes and dreams of a generation poised on the cusp of the unknown. It was an event that promised a journey to celestial bodies and a journey into the heart of human potential.

6.1 THE MOON LANDING PARTY THAT WASN'T

Astronomical Anticipation

The stage was set in a modest living room, the furniture pushed aside to make room for neighbors and friends, and a television set that hummed with static anticipation. The air was thick with excitement, a tangible buzz that resonated with the crackle of the TV, each flicker a prelude to the historic broadcast. Platters of carefully prepared snacks sat almost forgotten, as every eye was fixed on the screen, waiting for the moment when human feet would touch lunar soil. This gathering, a microcosm of millions worldwide, was united by a singular event that promised to transcend the ordinary, to elevate the human spirit to new heights.

Improvised Celebrations

Then, the unexpected: the screen blinked, faltered, and succumbed to silence. Technical difficulties, an all too human hiccup on this day of superhuman achievement, left the room suspended in a collective gasp. Yet, the absence of visuals could not dim the luminosity of the moment. What followed was a testament to the resilience of joy and the power of shared experience. The group, initially adrift in disappointment, found solace in improvisation. Stories began to fill the void, personal anecdotes of where they were when the mission launched and what the promise of space exploration meant to each. A guitar was found, and songs of the era, those hymns of hope and exploration, filled the room, transforming the gathering into a celebration, not of what was missed but of what was shared.

Stellar Memories

As the evening unfolded, the room became a vessel for memories, each tale a star in the constellation of the collective experience. One recounted a childhood dream of becoming an astronaut, and another shared a letter written to NASA, filled with the earnest curiosity of youth. Personal yet universal stories wove together the fabric of the evening, a tapestry enriched by the threads of individual journeys. Though unseen, the moon landing was felt—a palpable presence that inspired and reminded those gathered of the vastness of human ambition and the intimate connections that sustain us through disappointment and triumph.

Unified by the Moon

In reflection, the absence of the broadcast became inconsequential, a footnote in an evening that epitomized the essence of community. The gathering, though convened to witness history, became history itself—a testament to the enduring power of human connection. It underscored a profound truth: moments of collective anticipation, even when unfulfilled in the manner expected, can forge bonds that resonate with the strength of shared experience. The moon landing, an event that promised to elevate humanity to new realms, achieved its aim not through the missed visuals but through the unity it inspired. It was a reminder that in the vast tapestry of human endeavor, the threads of joy, resilience, and communal spirit bind us and elevate us to the stars, even when our eyes remain fixed on the ground.

Visual Element: The Threads That Bind Us

A collage, a visual symphony of the era, captures the essence of the moon landing party that wasn't. Photos of living rooms across the globe, filled with eager faces turned towards flickering screens, are interwoven with images of the moon, that celestial body that beckoned. Quotes from those who gathered, their words a testament to the power of the moment, frame the collage, each sentence a reminder of the unity forged in the crucible of anticipation. This visual narrative invites the viewer to step into the shoes of those who gathered, to feel the pulse of shared excitement, and to reflect on the enduring bonds formed in the simple act of coming together.

6.2 ELVIS HAS LEFT THE BUILDING...OR HAS HE?

A stir begins in the heart of a small town, where the days blend into each other with the comfortable predictability of a well-loved song. It's subtle at first, a murmur that sweeps through the streets like a gentle breeze, carrying the promise of something both nostalgic and refreshingly novel. The local community center, typically hosting quaint gatherings and weekly bingo nights, announces an event that quickens the town's pulse: an Elvis impersonation contest. The news spread from neighbor to neighbor with a fervor that belies the sleepy demeanor of the city, igniting a fire of excitement and casting a spotlight on the enduring influence of the King of Rock 'n' Roll.

The King's Influence

From the outset, it's clear this is no ordinary competition. It transcends age, drawing participants from every generation, from those who swayed to the strains of "Heartbreak Hotel" in their youth to those who know Elvis more as an icon than a man. Each contestant, armed with sequined jumpsuits and pomaded hair, steps into the spotlight as a performer and torchbearer of a legacy that refuses to dim. Rehearsals, once solitary endeavors, evolve into communal gatherings. The local diner, its jukebox now a shrine to Elvis hits, becomes a rehearsal stage, where tips on perfecting the hip swivel are exchanged over milkshakes and laughter.

Suspicious Minds

As the contest approaches, the atmosphere thickens with anticipation and, curiously, a hint of espionage. Participants, driven by a mix of admiration for Elvis and the competitive spirit of the contest, begin to eye each other with a playful suspicion reminiscent of the song "Suspicious Minds." The local barber sees a surge in requests for Elvis's iconic pompadour, each customer casting furtive glances around the shop, wary of revealing their secret weapon for the contest. Wardrobe malfunctions are whispered about with the gravity of state secrets, and the air is electric with the buzz of conspiracy theories about hidden talents and surprise performances. This crescendo of antics, suspicion, and laughter serves as a prelude to the main event, a symphony of preparation harmonizing the community in a shared excitement.

Heartbreak Hotel

On the contest day, the community center transforms into a vibrant tableau of Elvises (or Elvii, as some affectionately argue), each variant of the King a testament to the breadth of his impact.

The performances unfold with a blend of earnestness and humor. This tribute oscillates between poignant renditions of "Love Me Tender" and riotous interpretations of "Jailhouse Rock." Amid the sequins and song, something remarkable happens. The competitive edges soften, replaced by a collective embrace of the joy and absurdity of the moment. Laughter, shared between contestants and audiences, bridges the gap between performance and fellowship. In the so-called "Heartbreak Hotel," unexpected friendships are forged here, the shared admiration for Elvis acting as a catalyst for connections that extend beyond the stage, reminding all present of the communal spirit of music and the unifying power of shared admiration.

A Legacy Lives On

As the last note fades and the final hip swivel comes to rest, the contest concludes, but the reverberations of the event echo through the community. Elvis, or rather the myriad interpretations of him, leaves a mark that is felt long after the community center's lights dim. While centered around the emulation of a cultural icon, the contest reveals the depth of Elvis's influence, not just as a musician but as a figure who embodies the joy, resilience, and flair for the drama that characterizes the human spirit. It's a realization that the essence of Elvis, his ability to bring people together through the power of music and performance, endures woven into the fabric of the community's identity.

In the aftermath, as stories of the contest become part of the town's lore, shared over dinners and across generations, the legacy of Elvis persists, a reminder of the timeless appeal of music and the enduring capacity for joy to unite and uplift. Through laughter, song, and the occasional suspicious mind, the community discovers that while the King may have left the building, his spirit, his zest for life, and his ability to inspire joy and unity remain very much alive, a testament to the power of cultural icons to transcend time and space, binding us together in a shared human experience that defies the ages.

6.3 THE MYSTERY OF THE MISSING TV REMOTE: A 90S SAGA

In an era before digital omnipresence encroached upon the fabric of daily existence, a singular device reigned supreme in the living room's hierarchy of gadgets: the television remote. Its disappearance one languid summer afternoon set the stage for a family escapade that spiraled into a delightful conundrum, sparking an unplanned foray into the annals of family lore. This seemingly mundane incident unraveled into a narrative rich with intrigue, laughter, and a gentle nod to the simplicity of bygone days.

Domestic Detective

The initial realization of the remote's absence descended upon the household with the subtlety of a sitcom cliffhanger. Queries of its whereabouts bounced from room to room, met with shrugs and bemused denials, painting a picture of domestic tranquility disturbed. As the hours waned, the search intensified, morphing from casual inquiries to a full-blown inquisition. Sofas were upturned, cushions deposed in a flurry of feathers, and bookshelves interrogated, each nook and

cranny scrutinized under the increasingly des-
perate gaze of the family's self-appointed sleuths.
While fraught with the frustration of the elusive,
this quest became a source of mirth, each misstep
and false lead adding a layer of comedy to the
day's proceedings.

Clues and Chaos

Amidst the chaos, accusations flew, veiled in jest
yet tinged with the slight sting of suspicion. The
dog, an unwitting bystander, found itself the sub-
ject of scrutiny, its every move watched for signs
of guilt or, more implausibly, the sudden regurgi-
tation of the coveted object. Siblings long inured
to the art of blame-shifting crafted alibis with the
creativity of seasoned novelists, weaving tales of
innocence marred only by their implausibility.
Yet, within this whirlwind of speculation and
comedic investigation, moments of laughter bubbled to the surface, piercing the frustration with
the lightness of shared amusement.

Technological Time Capsule

As the day surrendered to the inevitability of night, the television, its screen dark and unyielding, stood as a silent monument to simpler times. The absence of the remote, while a source of momentary disarray, cast a spotlight on the stark contrast between then and now. In an age where digital devices command attention with the persistence of a seasoned courtier, the notion of a single missing remote paralyzing the evening's entertainment seems almost quaint. This saga, played out in the arena of family life, served as an unintentional time capsule, a reminder of days when entertainment was not a solitary pursuit but a shared experience, bounded not by the limitless realms of streaming but by the unity of a single screen.

Found Memories

The discovery of the remote, nestled in the unlikely embrace of the fridge's vegetable crisper, brought with it not just the resolution of the mystery but a pause for reflection. The laughter that greeted its return was tinged with the warmth of nostalgia, a recognition of the joy found in life's unplanned detours. This incident, trivial as it might have seemed, underscored the essence of family life before the dawn of the smartphone era —days characterized by the simplicity of shared moments, the richness of collective laughter, and the unspoken bond that forms in the pursuit of a common goal, even one as prosaic as locating a lost remote.

In this light, the saga of the missing remote transcends its humble beginnings, emerging as a narrative imbued with the charm of reminiscence and the gentle reminder of the value inherent in the mundane. It stands as a testament to the days when technology, while present, served as a backdrop to the drama of daily life rather than its focal point, reminding us of the beauty found in simplicity and the enduring power of family bonds forged in the crucible of shared experience and nurtured in the laughter that echoes through the years.

As we close this chapter, we carry forward the tale of a lost remote and the reflection on the essence of connectivity in its most human form. The laughter, the shared moments of frivolity, and the warmth of family life encapsulate the true spirit of togetherness, a theme that resonates through the ages, reminding us that at the heart of our stories are the simple joys that bind us. Onward, we move to further tales and reflections, each chapter a step deeper into exploring life's beautifully ordinary moments.

CHAPTER 7

THE TAPESTRY OF COMPANIONSHIP

In the dance of life, where Laughter is the music, unexpected missteps often lead to the most joyous twirls. Imagine a quiet evening that turns into an impromptu gathering of tales and chuckles, akin to those spontaneous rain showers on a sunny day that leave the world refreshed and glistening. In these moments, amid the chaos of plans gone awry and the serendipity of unanticipated joy, the essence of true companionship blooms, its roots deepening not despite but because of the unpredictability of life's rhythm.

7.1 THE GREAT BINGO HEIST

The Plan

A plot was quietly brewing in the heart of a community where Bingo nights were the pinnacle of entertainment—drawing crowds with the promise of camaraderie over competition. Not one born of malice but of mischief, conceived over cups of lukewarm tea and the shared desire to break the monotony of predictable outcomes. The target? The weekly Bingo game. The mission? To ensure a beloved member, notorious for her spectacular losing streak, finally tasted victory. The conspirators, a motley crew of longtime friends, devised a strategy brimming with elaborate distractions. From strategically timed coughing fits to the subtle misplacement of markers, the plan was a masterpiece of chaos, intended to gently skew the game in their friend's favor.

Unexpected Allies

What unfolded next was a comedy of errors that no rehearsal could have prepared them for. The simple act of a misplaced marker became the Butterfly Effect in action, leading to a cascade of events that roped in bystanders as unwitting accomplices. The local baker, attending his first Bingo night in hopes of relaxing after a day of wrestling with rebellious sourdough, found himself embroiled in the scheme. In attempting to return what he thought was a dropped marker, he inadvertently became the linchpin in a distraction that veered off course, resulting in confusion and misplaced Bingo cards. The chaos, while unintended, wove a thread of connection through the room, turning competitors into co-conspirators, each caught in the web of a plan spiraling delightfully out of control.

The Heist Unfolds

As the evening progressed, the heist, in all its orchestrated disarray, unfolded with the elegance of a dance where the dancers forget their steps yet find themselves in perfect sync. Bingo calls were missed, markers were dropped in a symphony of clatters, and the room buzzed with confusion that masked the undercurrent of shared Laughter. The plan, veering wildly from its original course, became an exercise in improvisation. Each mishap, rather than a setback, added to the crescendo of mirth that filled the room. The game, long held as a bastion of quiet concentration, transformed into a lively tableau of human connection, a reminder of the joy found in collective spontaneity.

The Prize

Ultimately, the prize, a modest but coveted hamper of local treats, did not reach the intended victor. Instead, amidst the Laughter and the gentle chaos, a newcomer, the baker, won it, whose unintended role in the evening's escapade had endeared him to all. The revelation that the prize was not the basket of goods but the experience itself dawned on the conspirators. The value lay in the shared Laughter, the warmth of friendship, and the realization that sometimes, the best-laid plans lead not to their intended destination but to a place of unexpected joy and deeper connections.

This evening, a tapestry of mishaps and mirth, underscored a fundamental truth about companionship: the strongest bonds are forged not in the flawless execution of plans but in the shared journey through the unexpected. Much like life, companionship thrives not on predictability but on the capacity to find Laughter in the chaos and embrace the detours that lead us to moments of unanticipated joy.

7.2 THE FRIENDSHIP QUILT WITH TOO MANY COOKS

In the heart of a tight-knit community, a novel idea blossomed, seeking to weave the individual threads of friendship into a tangible tapestry of memories and personalities. This endeavor took shape as a friendship quilt. On this patchwork canvas, each square would echo the essence of a different friend, a kaleidoscope of stories and traits stitched together with care and Laughter. The project, conceived in the spirit of unity and creativity, soon became a vibrant battlefield where aesthetics clashed, humor flourished, and the diversity of friendships was celebrated in every thread and color choice.

This communal artwork was initiated by a gathering that bore more resemblance to a diplomatic summit than a crafting session. Friends came armed with fabrics, each piece a bearer of significance, and ideas that ranged from the sublime to the whimsical. As the proposals unfolded, it became evident that the quilt would be no ordinary creation. Design choices collided in a jumble of preferences; where one saw the elegance of minimalism, another envisioned a riot of colors. Themes emerged, from the abstract to the literal, each vying for a place in the quilt's narrative. This cacophony of creative inputs, rather than a smooth chorus, became the project's first note of true camaraderie, a testament to the richness that lies in diversity.

As the quilt began to take shape, the process revealed itself to be less about the perfection of each square and more about the stories each piece told. Missteps were frequent; a square might shrink in the wash, or a color chosen in solitary confidence would clash outrageously when placed beside its neighbors. Yet, each error became a thread in the quilt's larger story, a moment of shared problem-solving that often ended in Laughter rather than frustration. Friends found themselves negotiating not just about designs but about the essence of their memories and relationships. A square intended to represent resilience might be too dark, a piece meant to convey joy too gaudy. Yet, in this negotiation, a deeper understanding emerged, a give-and-take that mirrored the dynamics of their friendships. With each square and stitch, the quilt became a testament to the beauty of compromise and the strength found in acknowledging and celebrating differences.

The unveiling of the quilt was an event that mirrored the vibrancy and warmth of the friendships it represented. Gathered around the completed masterpiece, the group found themselves admiring their handiwork and recounting the journey that had led them to this moment. Each square, now a harmonious part of the whole, sparked anecdotes and reminiscences, from the debates over fabric choices to the Laughter that followed each crafting mishap. With its jumble of styles and themes, this eclectic beauty of the quilt stood as a vibrant symbol of the group's collective spirit, a patchwork of personalities that, when woven together, created a tapestry of enduring warmth and connection.

In the Laughter and stories that filled the room, the quilt ceased to be just a collection of fabric and thread. It transformed into a living narrative, a woven record of friendships that thrived on diversity, understanding, and the shared joy of creation. The project, which began as an idea to encapsulate individual personalities in a communal artwork, evolved into a journey that mirrored the complexities and joys of friendship itself. Through every choice of color, every adjustment of design, and every stitch that bound the squares into a cohesive whole, the friends navigated the nuances of their relationships, finding in the challenges of collaboration a deeper appreciation for the unique qualities that each brought to the tapestry of their shared experiences.

The friendship quilt, with its myriad squares and the Laughter sewn into its seams, stood as a testament to the enduring bonds forged in the fires of creativity and compromise. It was a reminder that the most beautiful creations emerge not from uniformity but from the willingness to embrace and celebrate differences, to weave together the disparate threads of personalities into a work of art that reflects the depth and richness of human connection. In the end, the quilt was more than just a piece of handiwork; it was a symbol of the strength and beauty of friendships that, like the squares of the quilt, are each unique yet bound together in a pattern of enduring love and Laughter.

7.3 THE SECRET LANGUAGE OF FRIENDS

In the heart of a small community where time meandered like a gentle stream, a pact was born among a circle of friends, a whimsical agreement to weave their own covert tapestry of communication. This pact, conceived in the glow of a firefly-lit evening, was more than a mere child's play; it was a declaration of unity, a linguistic rebellion against the mundane. They embarked on this endeavor with the zeal of alchemists; each word they concocted was a secret ingredient in the elixir of their friendship. This language, a mosaic of invented words and phrases, became their fortress of solitude, impervious to the uninitiated. Yet, the very fabric of this secret speech, designed to unify, occasionally cast shadows of confusion on those beyond its walls, stitching a pattern of humorous misunderstandings into the quilt of community life.

Invented Languages

The invention of this language was a task approached with solemnity and a spark of mischief. Each term was crafted with care, a reflection of shared experiences and inside jokes that had cemented their bond. A word might be born from a misadventure at the local fair, another from the peculiar habit of a beloved pet. This language was their archive, a living museum of moments that had folded into the creases of their camaraderie. It evolved, a living entity that grew with each gathering, each shared victory and setback. Yet, its richness, woven from the exclusive tapestry of their fellowship, often draped a veil of perplexity over interactions with the community, leading to sequences of events unfurled with the unpredictability of a summer storm.

The Power of Understanding

This language was a key within the circle, unlocking deeper layers of connection and understanding. A single, seemingly nonsensical phrase could evoke peals of Laughter or a knowing nod, a testament to the depth of their bond. It was a linguistic dance, each step, each word, an echo of shared history and mutual affection. While perplexing to outsiders, this secret language was the glue that bound them, a constant reminder of the sanctuary they had found in one another's company. Yet, the exclusivity of their communication, while never intended to alienate, occasionally erected barriers where bridges were meant to stand, a paradox that lent strength and vulnerability to the fabric of their friendship.

Lost in Translation

An incident at the annual community picnic served as a pivotal chapter in the saga of their secret language. Tasked with organizing the event, the friends saw it as an opportunity to infuse the gathering with the unique spirit of their group. Instructions for games and activities conveyed in their cryptic vernacular were met with bemused glances and polite, albeit confused, nods. The scavenger hunt, a picnic highlight, became an unintentional comedy of errors. Clues, veiled in the cloak of their private language, led participants not to the hidden treasures but on a wild chase through the park, interpreting signs and landmarks through a lens of bewildering creativity. The day, while not unfolding as planned, became a tapestry of Laughter and light-hearted bewilderment, a shared adventure that, despite its deviations, drew the community closer, the humor of the situation a bridge over the chasm of confusion.

The Inclusion

In the aftermath of the picnic, a realization dawned upon the group. The beauty of their language, while a source of joy and unity among them, held the potential to transcend the boundaries of their circle. An evening was set under the same firefly-lit sky where their pact was first made to open the doors of their linguistic sanctuary to the community. The gathering was a symposium, a celebration of inclusion where the secret language was shared, not as a tool of division but as an invitation to Laughter and companionship. The event unfolded with the fluidity of a river breaking its banks, the community embracing the quirky vernacular enthusiastically. Free from the constraints of confusion, Laughter filled the air as the language took on new life, adopted and adapted by the wider circle. This act of inclusion was a testament to the adaptive nature of friendship, a reminder that joy, when shared, multiplies, weaving a more robust, vibrant tapestry of community connection.

In this light, the chapter on the secret language of friends stands as a parable of the complexities and triumphs of companionship. It underscores the beauty in creating private worlds, the strength drawn from shared understanding, and the joy that blossoms when these worlds open their gates. The friends illuminated the path from exclusivity to inclusivity through Laughter, confusion, and the eventual sharing of their secret speech. This journey mirrors the broader human endeavor to find a connection in a world rich with diversity.

As we fold this tale into the fabric of our narrative, let us carry forward the melody of Laughter that resonates through these stories. This is a reminder of the simple yet profound truth that in sharing our quirks and stories, we find the threads that bind us all, leading us into the next chapter of our shared journey.

CHAPTER 8

THE WHISK AND THE WHIMSY

In a world where the kitchen often becomes the heart of the home, a family found themselves at the helm of an unexpected adventure, stirred not by the usual recipe of daily meals but by the sweet and savory challenge of a local pie contest. This wasn't just any culinary competition; it was a battle of buttery crusts and sumptuous fillings that promised glory to the tastiest pie and the most cunning bakers. In this tale of competitive baking, secret recipes, and the inevitable chaos of contest day, we discover that sometimes, the actual recipe for happiness isn't written down but baked into the moments we share.

8.1 THE PIE CONTEST CAPER

Competitive Baking

Imagine a sunny Saturday morning, the air filled with the scent of blooming flowers and freshly cut grass, setting the stage for a baking contest that would soon become the talk of the town. The Smith family, known in their neighborhood for their culinary prowess and spirited sense of competition, saw the announcement of the contest not just as a call to action but as a gauntlet thrown down. Each member, from the matriarch with her decades of pie-baking wisdom to the youngest, a whiz with flavors, entered the fray determined to claim the title of best pie maker. The kitchen became a battleground of flour clouds and sugar spills, where strategies were as crucial as the recipes.

Secret Recipes and Sabotage

As the contest loomed, the family's competitive nature turned toward espionage. The once open book of family recipes became a vault of secrets, each member guarding their pie recipe with a zeal reminiscent of a cat circling its territory. Whispers of "apple or cherry?" met with mischievous grins and evasive answers. Attempts to peek at each other's ingredient lists led to comedic sabotage efforts: sugar was subtly replaced with salt, and crucial spices were hidden away. The kitchen, a place of shared meals and Laughter, now mirrored a scene straight out of a sitcom, where each attempt to gain the upper hand only added to the cacophony of mishaps and misunderstandings.

The Taste Test

Contest day arrived with the festival fanfare, the air tinged with anticipation, and the sweet aroma of pies in their final moments of glory in the oven. The Smiths, armed with their secret weapons cloaked in pastry, entered the community center with heads held high, only to find their carefully laid plans crumble like an overworked dough. Amidst the hustle and bustle, pies were mixed up, names swapped, and the judges, a panel of local celebrities, and culinary experts were left bewildered but delighted by the variety of flavors and stories each pie presented. The contest, intended to display individual skill, transformed into a symphony of errors and Laughter, where the true challenge lay not in the baking but in keeping track of which pie belonged to whom.

Sweet Victory

In a twist that none could have predicted, the contest ended not with a single Smith standing triumphant but with the entire family called to the stage. Though entered separately, their pies had been judged as a collective masterpiece of flavors and innovation. This decision baffled the family as much as it did the audience. The judges, amused by the mix-up and impressed by the quality across the board, declared the Smith family the contest winners. The unexpected victory served as a gentle reminder of the strength found in unity, in the shared laughs over misplaced pies, and the collaborative efforts to outdo each other that, inadvertently, led to their collective win. The recipe for happiness, it turned out, wasn't about guarding secrets or striving for individual glory but about the joy of coming together and celebrating each other's strengths and quirks.

Visual Element: The Pie Contest Family Album

A scrapbook-style collection of photos captures the essence of the Smith family's journey through the pie contest, from candid shots of flour-covered faces and the controlled chaos of their kitchen battleground to the humorous mishaps of contest day and their final, unexpected victory. Each image is accompanied by short, light-hearted captions that invite the viewer into the story, offering a glimpse into the Laughter, the trials, and the sweet success of the day. This visual narrative commemorates the family's adventure. It serves as a heartwarming reminder of the beauty of shared endeavors and the unexpected paths to happiness.

In this chapter, the kitchen becomes more than a place of culinary creation; it emerges as a battleground where the weapons are whisks and the victories are sweet. The tale of the Smith family and their pie contest caper reveals the layers of competition, camaraderie, and the unexpected twists that blend to create the rich recipe of life. Through their story, we are reminded that the most memorable moments often arise from the simplest ingredients: Laughter, love, and a willingness to embrace the whimsy of the whisk.

8.2 THE CASE OF THE MISPLACED DENTURES

In the quietude that typically embraced the household on a lazy Sunday afternoon, an air of mystery unfurled its wings, casting shadows of bewilderment across the faces of the family. It began with Grandpa, his usual jovial demeanor clouded by perplexity, announcing the inexplicable vanishing of his dentures. Such an essential yet mundane item's disappearance set the stage for an investigation that would soon spiral into a family endeavor marked by absurdity and revelation.

A Dental Mystery

The initial reaction was disbelief, peppered with humor that finds its roots in the family's shared history of misadventures. Yet, as the reality of the situation sank in, a search operation unfolded with an earnestness that belied the comedic undertone of the problem. From the depths of the living room couch to the less-trodden corners of the attic, no stone was left unturned, no cushion unprobed. Grandpa, a revered and loved figure, watched as his progeny transformed into detectives, their methods unorthodox, guided more by whimsy than logic.

Clues and Confusion

The pursuit of the missing dentures led the family down a labyrinth of false leads and red herrings. A trail of breadcrumbs, in this case, misplaced items from previous searches, muddied the waters, leading to wild theories that bordered on the fantastical. The dog's newfound interest in a particular corner of the garden was misconstrued as a clue, leading to an impromptu excavation that unearthed nothing more than a long-forgotten toy. The youngest of the clan, imbued with imagination as vast as the open sea, posited the theory of a magpie's involvement, captivated by the shine of the dentures. This hypothesis led to a brief but earnest stakeout of the backyard. Each misstep, while adding layers of confusion, wove into the fabric of the day a sense of camaraderie and shared purpose that transcended the frustration of the hunt.

Unexpected Discovery

The denouement of this familial saga came not in the form of a dramatic revelation but as a stumbled-upon truth found in the least expected places. The dentures, those elusive artifacts of daily necessity, were discovered nestled within the serene confines of the bread box, an innocent bystander in this comedy of errors. As it turned out, the culprit was Grandpa himself, who, in a moment of forgetfulness, had deemed it the perfect hiding spot from a perceived dental nemesis in a dream the night before. This revelation, absurd as it was, brought forth gales of Laughter. This kind bubbles up from the belly and spills over in uncontrollable mirth.

Laughter and Lessons

The Laughter that filled the house in the wake of the discovery was a balm, soothing the edges of embarrassment and frustration that had tinged the day's earlier endeavors. It served as a reminder that the fabric of family life is embroidered with moments of forgetfulness and folly, each thread as crucial to the tapestry as those woven from love and shared joy. The incident of the misplaced dentures, while a minor blip in the grand scheme, underscored the unpredictable nature of family life, where mysteries and misadventures are but opportunities for Laughter and for forging deeper bonds. In the end, as the sun dipped below the horizon, casting a golden glow that seemed to laugh along with them, the family found itself richer, not for having solved the mystery, but for the journey they had undertaken together, a testament to the enduring power of love, patience, and the shared Laughter that dances through the rooms of home alive with the whimsy of being together.

8.3 A FAMILY REUNION TO REMEMBER

Planning Pandemonium

In the intricate dance of orchestrating a family reunion, the initial steps often resemble less a graceful ballet and more a spirited jig, replete with toe-stepping and out-of-sync rhythms. Amidst this whirlwind of well-intentioned chaos, the Thompson clan found themselves, each member armed with opinions as varied as their personalities, attempting to sculpt from the ether of ideas a gathering that would span generations and geographies. Emails flew like arrows, each laden with suggestions ranging from the nostalgic—picnics in the park of yesteryears—to the novel—a virtual reality tour of ancestral lands. This cacophony of voices, each echoing the desire for perfection, only served to weave a tapestry of complication, a testament to the family's diversity and strength. Yet, within this apparent disarray, a blueprint of the reunion slowly emerged, a testament not to the triumph of one idea but to the amalgamation of many.

The Arrival

On the long-anticipated day, as the sun rose with the promise of memories to be made, the Thompson homestead transformed into a hive of activity. Cars rolled in, each disgorging its occupants like clowns from a circus vehicle, a parade of relatives spanning the spectrum from Great Aunt Edna, with her penchant for cheek-pinching, to little Timmy, whose energy seemed as boundless as the summer day. Luggage, laden with gifts and garb for the weekend's festivities, piled up in the foyer, a mountain of anticipation. Hugs were exchanged, each embracing a bridge over the rivers of time and distance that had flowed since their last gathering. Laughter punctuated the air, a melody that spoke of joy and reunion, even as the controlled chaos of arrivals hinted at the undercurrent of complexity that defines every family.

Reunion Revelations

As the day unfolded, the reunion became a canvas upon which the Thompsons painted with broad strokes of emotion and experience. Stories long buried beneath the sediment of time bubbled to the surface, shared over plates of food that seemed as much a part of the family as those gathered around the table. In the sanctuary of shared space, revelations came to light here—secrets that sparked surprise, confessions that drew tears, and anecdotes that incited roars of Laughter. Old grievances, those petty squabbles that had once seemed insurmountable, melted away under the warmth of rekindled connections. Bonds were fortified by the recollection of shared pasts and the forging of new memories, a mosaic of the moment each would carry with them.

The Perfect Imperfection

As the reunion drew to a close, with the sun dipping below the horizon, painting the sky with strokes of crimson and gold, a moment of collective reflection enveloped the gathering. The realization dawned, soft as the evening light, that the beauty of their time together lay not in the seamless execution of plans or the absence of mishap. Instead, it resided in the imperfections, those moments of unexpected vulnerability, of Laughter born of error, and of plans gone awry that led to adventures unscripted. This gathering, marked by the cacophony of planning, the whirlwind of arrivals, and the tapestry of revelations, was a microcosm of life itself—unpredictable, sometimes messy, but immeasurably enriched by the presence of each soul that formed the Thompson clan. Ultimately, the joy found in simply being together, in embracing the chaos and the calm, would linger long after the last car departed and the final dish was washed. The reunion, a testament to the enduring vibrancy of familial bonds, stood as a beacon to the Thompsons, a reminder that in the aggregation of their imperfections lay their perfection, a family united not just by blood but by the shared journey through the spectrum of human experience.

In the narrative of our lives, the chapters filled with Laughter shared meals, and the warmth of togetherness resonate with the deepest timbre. The Thompson family reunion, with its planning pandemonium, its parade of arrivals, and the tapestry of revelations, serves as a vibrant reminder of the beauty inherent in the chaos of coming together. As we turn the page to explore new stories, let us carry forward the melody of shared Laughter and the light of familial love, the true north stars that guide us through the dance of life.

CHAPTER 9

TRIUMPHS IN THE TWILIGHT

A delicate and unique snowflake can be the harbinger of change, transforming landscapes and plans with its silent descent. So it was on a day that dawned clear and cold, promising nothing more than the gentle passage of time, an unexpected snowstorm began its dance, a ballet of chaos upon a stage of senior expectations. The seniors, a lively group with plans etched in anticipation for an event long-awaited, found themselves at the mercy of nature's whimsy. The snow, relentlessly pursuing silence and stillness, blanketed the world in white, severing connections and challenging the resolve of those it ensnared.

9.1 THE SNOWSTORM THAT LED TO AN UNEXPECTED ADVENTURE

The Challenge

As the snow piled high, obscuring paths and erasing the familiar contours of the world, the seniors faced a dilemma that tested their patience and their spirit. The event they had looked forward to, a gathering of minds and hearts, seemed a distant dream, smothered under the weight of winter's unexpected gift. Faced with the prospect of isolation, a lesser spirit might have conceded defeat, yet within the hearts of these seasoned souls burned a fire undimmed by the cold, a determination that the snow, for all its might, could not quench.

Ingenious Solutions

Resourcefulness, often born of necessity, took the helm as the seniors crafted plans as unique as the snowflakes that barred their way. Kitchen trays, relics of meals shared and enjoyed, found new life as makeshift sleds, their surfaces slick against the snow, transforming a burden into a source of joy. Laughter, a universal language undimmed by age, echoed through the air as races ensued, not for glory but for the sheer delight of movement and companionship. Snowshoes, cobbled together from garden tools and determination, became the vehicles of exploration, carrying the group through a world transformed, where every step was an act of defiance against the quiet insistence of the snow.

Unexpected Journey

The world, seen through the veil of falling snow, offered a vision of beauty stark and pure, a reminder of nature's power to both hinder and awe. As the seniors ventured forth, their progress marked by Laughter and the crunch of snow underfoot, they discovered a world reborn in ice and silence, a canvas upon which the mundane was painted with the brush of the extraordinary. Streets, once familiar, now bore the mark of the untamed, with trees bowing under the weight of snow, their branches like hands raised in surrender to the sky. The journey, intended to bridge the distance between isolation and connection, became a voyage of discovery, where every turn revealed a landscape undreamed of, a world waiting to be explored.

Warmth in the Cold

Arrival, when it came, was not at the destination they had envisioned but at a haven forged from necessity and the warmth of human connection. A local hall, its doors thrown open in welcome, became the sanctuary from the storm, a place where the cold was banished by the heat of shared stories and the glow of companionship. Here, gathered around tables laden with im-promptu offerings, the seniors found nothing more profound than the event they had planned: a sense of community and belonging, a warmth that the cold could not touch. It was a realization that the journey, with its trials and Laughter, detours, and discoveries, held more meaning than the destination. The storm, for all its disruption, had led them not astray but to a deeper understanding of the bonds that connect the triumphs born of adversity and the joy found in the unexpected twists of life's path.

Visual Element: A Snowy Tapestry

A series of photographs captures the essence of the adventure, from the initial dismay at the snow's arrival to the joy of sled races and the beauty of the snow-clad world. Each image, framed by the seniors' Laughter and determination, tells a story of triumph over the unexpected, a visual testament to the power of community and the warmth that resides in the human heart, even in the coldest of times.

In this narrative of snow and resilience, the seniors remind us that life, with all its unpredictability, holds moments of beauty and connection waiting to be discovered. Through their eyes, we see not the obstacles but the opportunities, not the cold but the warmth that comes from shared experiences and the Laughter that echoes through the snow, a melody of triumph in the twilight of life.

9.2 THE COMEBACK OF THE SENIOR SOFTBALL LEAGUE

Under a canopy of skepticism, a narrative unfolds, where a group of spirited seniors, clad in the vibrancy of their team jerseys, confronts the tide of doubt cast by the younger onlookers. Their intent, a bold stride into competitive softball, was met not with encouragement but a chorus of disbelief. The notion that age could diminish the fervor or the agility required for the sport became a shadow that trailed their every step, a challenge not just to their physical capabilities but to the essence of their resolve. Yet, within this crucible of doubt, determination found its flame, kindling a fire that would soon illuminate the path to an unexpected resurgence.

In the days that followed, the air around the makeshift practice field, a patchwork of grass and dreams on the outskirts of the community park, vibrated with the echoes of a renaissance. Training, a term that barely encapsulated the fusion of Laughter, sweat, and occasional mishits that characterized their sessions, became the crucible in which stereotypes were dismantled. Each swing of the bat, each dive for a stray ball, wove into their preparation a narrative of defiance, a visual sonnet to the agelessness of passion. The methods employed, a blend of traditional drills and inventive exercises that often borrowed from the comedy of errors, served to hone their skills and fortify the camaraderie that pulsed at the heart of their team. This montage of persever-ance, underscored by the rhythmic thud of balls meeting gloves and the steady cadence of foot-steps on the diamond, painted a portrait of a team undeterred by the calendar's dictations. This collective spirit soared beyond the confines of expectation.

Game day dawned, a crescendo in their sym-phony of preparation, the field aglow with the anticipation of competition and the unspoken promise of vindication. The stands, a mosaic of spectators whose interest had been piqued by tales of the seniors' audacity, bore witness to a spectacle that transcended the boundaries of a mere softball game. Each inning unfurled with the unpredictability of a story yet unwritten, where the seniors, their movements a testament to the meticulousness of their training, navigated the diamond with a blend of precision and grace unexpected by those who had cast them in the role of underdogs. Plays, marked by the strategic acumen honed over a lifetime of experience and the physical prowess that belied the years, unfolded with a fluidity that silenced the murmurs of doubt. The ball, propelled by their determination, became a beacon of their capabilities; each hit a rebuttal to the skepticism that had once clouded their endeavor.

As the final inning waned, the scoreboard told a tale of triumph, not just of scored runs but broken barriers. The seniors, their jerseys stained with the evidence of their exertion and their faces alight with the glow of accomplishment, emerged not just as victors in the game but as champions of a cause more significant than the sum of its innings. The applause that cascaded from the stands, a symphony of recognition and newfound respect, enveloped the team in a cloak of validation, a tangible acknowledgment of their prowess and the futility of underestimation. This moment crystallized in the collective memory of those present, served as a beacon to others, a testament to the boundlessness of human potential and the indomitable spirit that thrives within those who dare to challenge the constraints of age and expectation.

In this competition arena, where the crack of the bat against the ball echoed like a declaration of defiance, the seniors redefined the contours of possibility. Their journey, marked by the Laughter that punctuated their training and the determination that fueled their game, wove into the tapestry of the community a narrative of perseverance. This story transcends the confines of a softball field to resonate in the hearts of all who bear witness. This story, a mosaic of ambition, preparation, and triumph, stands as a testament to the enduring power of belief in oneself and in the collective strength of those united by a shared purpose, a reminder that the flame of competition burns as brightly within the twilight as it does in the dawn.

9.3 THE GARDEN THAT GREW MORE THAN JUST FLOWERS

In the heart of a community where the rhythm of life flowed with serene predictability, a seed of an idea took root in the mind of Mr. Thompson, a senior with a vision tinted with the hues of green and the vibrant colors of blooming flowers. His proposal of a community garden, a space where nature could be nurtured and a nurturer, encountered initial hesitations. Doubts sprouted like un-welcome weeds, fed by concerns over the feasibility of such an endeavor, the commitment it would require, and the challenge of trans-forming a neglected plot of land into a flour-ishing oasis.

Undeterred by the skepticism, Mr. Thompson's resolve mirrored the steadfastness of an oak. With patience, he addressed each doubt, his words painting a picture of a garden that was more than just a space for plants to grow—it was to be a haven for community spirit. In this place, gardening would sow seeds of connection among individuals. His infectious and unwavering en-thusiasm gradually eroded the walls of reluc-tance, drawing volunteers from their shells of doubt.

As shovels broke ground, the project faced its first actual test. The stubborn and unyielding soil seemed a reflection of the initial resistance the idea had met. Nutrient-poor and compacted, it was a canvas of challenge, yet under Mr. Thompson's guidance and the community's growing involvement, amendments were mixed in, each bag of compost and peat a testament to their collective determination. Rain, too, seemed to conspire against them, either by its absence or in deluges that threatened to drown their nascent efforts. Yet, every hurdle fortified their resolve, transforming obstacles into stepping stones. The garden became a lesson in resilience; each challenge surmounted a victory for the plants that slowly began to thrive and the community that did so alongside them.

With time, the garden blossomed, both literally and metaphorically. Rows of vegetables stood as a testament to the care and effort invested. At the same time, flowers added splashes of color, and their beauty was a daily reminder of the project's underlying purpose. This transformation was not confined to the garden alone; individuals who had once been mere acquaintances shared Laughter and stories over beds of lettuce and tomatoes, their bonds strengthening with each passing day. Once isolated by the invisible barriers of age and routine, seniors found a renewed sense of purpose and belonging in the garden. The youth, initially skeptical, now eagerly participated, their energy and enthusiasm infusing the project with vitality.

Harvest day arrived with a bounty of produce and a cornucopia of joy and unity. The garden, once a dream met with skepticism, now stood as a vibrant testimony to the power of community. It was a celebration of the fruits of their labor and the intangible harvest they had reaped: friendships forged in the shared soil of effort, laughter that had blossomed amidst the greenery, and a sense of accomplishment that stretched beyond the garden's fences. This success was measured not in the weight of the harvest but in the lightness of hearts and the warmth of smiles shared under the canopy of their achievement.

In this garden, every plant and flower that grew reflected the growth within each individual involved. It was a space where plants and people flourished, nurtured by the communal soil of support and care. The challenges faced, from the unyielding soil to the capricious weather, deepened their resilience, teaching them that obstacles could be overcome when faced together. In its lush verdancy, the garden was a testament to the beauty that arises when individuals unite, uniting in purpose and effort.

As the sun dipped below the horizon, casting long shadows across the garden that had grown more than just flowers, it was evident that this project had cultivated something far more decadent than expected. It had grown a community, binding them in a tapestry of greenery, effort, and shared joy. This endeavor, which had begun with a single seed of an idea, had blossomed into a legacy of unity and resilience, a reminder of the transformative power of coming together for a common cause.

In the fading light, as the community gathered to celebrate their collective achievement, they stood as individuals and as a testament to the enduring strength of communal bonds, nurtured in the soil of cooperation and blooming in the garden of shared triumphs. This garden, a once-dormant plot brought to life by the hands and hearts of those who believed in its potential, stood as a beacon of hope and unity, a vibrant reminder of what can be achieved when individuals unite to pursue a common goal.

As we turn the soil in this chapter, we carry forward the essence of growth, unity, and the joy discovered in the shared journey of transforming challenges into victories. In all its verdant glory, the garden stands as a symbol of what we can cultivate together, a testament to the power of community and the enduring beauty of working hand in hand towards a shared vision.

CHAPTER 10

MELODIES OF MISCHIEF AND MIRTH

A cruise ship, a bastion of leisure and luxury, glides gracefully over the ocean's vast expanse. Within its steel confines, a microcosm of society gathers—seniors, mainly, find themselves drawn to its promise of adventure and relaxation. It's here, amidst the tranquil sea and under the watchful gaze of the setting sun, that an evening of karaoke transforms into an unexpected odyssey of laughter, bonding, and self-discovery.

10.1 THE CRUISE SHIP KARAOKE FIASCO

Tuning Trouble

Imagine a karaoke machine's screen flickering to life, the first notes of a familiar tune warbling through the speakers. It's a senior's turn, a moment they've anticipated with excitement and trepidation. Stepping up, the microphone feels heavy, a beacon of attention. As the music swells, so does their courage, until a mischievous twist of fate—a wrong track plays, a song unfamiliar yet undeniably catchy. Expecting a classic ballad, the audience finds themselves serenaded with a peppy pop song. The initial shock quickly gives way to amusement as the undeterred senior embraces the mistake, their performance transforming into a spirited anthem that unites the room in laughter and applause. It's a reminder that sometimes, the best moments arise from the unplanned, the courage to continue despite the unexpected.

Lyric Lapses

A humorous twist often awaits in karaoke, where lyrics flash on screens as guides to would-be singers. Picture a senior, their glasses perched precariously, squinting at the words dancing before them. Misreads and misinterpretations ensue, turning timeless classics into sources of merriment. Imagine "dancing queen, young and sweet, only seventeen" becoming "dancing green, young and keen, only a submarine." Such delightful lapses transform the room, encouraging others to find joy in imperfection. This shared laughter echoes louder than the music.

Unexpected Duets

Karaoke, in its essence, is a solitary endeavor until it's not. A song, midway, falters—a senior's voice losing steam. From the audience, a voice rises, clear and confident, joining in an unplanned duet that bridges generations. A teen, perhaps, who rolled their eyes at the thought of spending an evening at a senior's karaoke, now stands side by side with their elder, voices melding in harmony. This alliance, born of spontaneity, becomes the highlight, a performance that transcends age and genre, reminding all present of the unifying power of music. It's a testament to the unexpected connections that music can foster, turning a solo journey into a collective celebration.

Encore Adventures

The night winds down, but the memories linger, buoyed by laughter and newfound friendships. Once hesitant, seniors now buzz with the excitement of stepping out of their comfort zones. Encouraged by the evening's misadventures, they vow to seize more spontaneous moments and find joy in the unexpected. Conversations flourish, and plans are made—perhaps a talent show next or a dance-off. The karaoke fiasco, rather than a moment of embarrassment, becomes a cherished memory, a stepping stone to future endeavors that embrace the thrill of the new.

Visual Element: A Night to Remember

A photo montage captures the essence of the evening. Images of seniors stepping up to the microphone, faces alight with laughter at lyrical slip-ups and unexpected duets that brought down the house. Each picture, framed with snippets of overheard comments and laughter, invites the viewer into the heart of the experience. It's a visual diary, a testament to the night when music and mischief wove a tapestry of connection, encouraging all to embrace life's unplanned melodies.

In this chapter, the cruise ship serves as more than a vessel on the sea; it becomes a crucible of human experience, where music, laughter, and the unexpected converge to create moments of genuine connection and joy. Through the karaoke fiasco, seniors rediscover the exhilaration of stepping into the unknown, finding harmony in the unexpected, and the laughter that ties them together, echoing long after the music fades.

10.2 LOST AT THE LOUVRE: A PARISIAN ESCAPADE

In the labyrinthine halls of the Louvre, awash with the light that filters through its glass pyramid, a contingent of spirited seniors found themselves momentarily adrift from their guided convoy. This detachment, far from a mishap, unfolded into an odyssey of discovery within the museum's venerable walls, where corridors whisper tales of epochs long past, and masterpieces gaze down upon visitors with timeless dignity. Undaunted by the prospect of navigating the world's largest museum unchaperoned, the seniors embraced this interlude as an opportunity for adventure, their footsteps echoing on marble floors as they ventured deeper into the artistic sanctum.

Artistic Wanderings

The initial disorientation soon gave way to exhilaration as the group, armed with nothing but their wits and a handful of museum maps, deciphered their path through the galleries. Each room revealed a new chapter in humanity's artistic endeavor, from the stoic faces of Egyptian sarcophagi to the tumultuous beauty of Renaissance canvases. The seniors, undeterred by the vastness of their surroundings, engaged with the art in a manner unbound by the conventions of guided tours. They lingered where curiosity beckoned, allowing the stories encapsulated in oil and marble to unfold at their own pace. This meandering route through the museum was less about the destination and more about the serendipity of discovery, each unexpected turn revealing treasures untold.

Historical Misinterpretations

Amidst their explorations, the seniors' interpretations of the artworks they encountered strayed delightfully from academic analyses, giving birth to a tapestry of tales woven from imagination and humor. A portrait's enigmatic smile led to speculation of clandestine lovers and hidden messages. At the same time, the dramatic poses of classical statues inspired whimsical narratives of ancient soap operas and mythological mishaps. These interpretations, shared among the group with a blend of earnestness and jest, caught the ears of nearby visitors, their amusement growing as they were drawn into the seniors' fanciful conjectures. This communal exchange of stories, rooted in the fanciful rather than the factual, transformed the gallery spaces into forums of laughter and camaraderie. Art became the backdrop for creating new, shared myths.

Cultural Connections

As they meandered, the seniors' paths intersected with those of travelers across the globe, each drawn to the Louvre by their quests for beauty and understanding. These crossings of trajectories blossomed into exchanges of anecdotes and recommendations, the seniors' vibrant tales of misadventure serving as bridges between cultures. Language barriers, rather than obstacles, became puzzles to solve together, with gestures and laughter serving as universal currencies of friendship. The museum, a crossroads of human history, thus transformed into a meeting place for present-day voyagers, each enriching the other's journey. The seniors, with their tales of artistic wanderings and historical misinterpretations, wove themselves into the larger narrative of the museum, their laughter a contemporary addition to its ancient halls.

Found Amongst the Art

The eventual reunion with their tour group was not marked by relief but by a tinge of wistfulness as the seniors bade farewell to their brief but intense foray into independence within the

Louvre's embrace. Yet, the experiences garnered, from the whimsical interpretations of art to the connections forged with strangers, imbued them with a sense of accomplishment and a wealth of stories to share. While informative, the guide's recounting of historical facts and artist biographies paled in comparison to the vibrant adventure the seniors had authored for themselves. They had not simply viewed the art; they had interacted with it, allowing it to catalyze creativity, connection, and joy. The Louvre, with its endless galleries and treasures, had offered them an unexpected gift: the realization that art is not just to be seen but to be experienced, its actual value lying in the memories created and the bonds strengthened in its presence.

In this Parisian escapade, the seniors discovered that sometimes, getting lost is not a misfortune but an invitation to adventure, a chance to see the world and its wonders from a new perspective. Their journey through the Louvre, marked by laughter, imagination, and unexpected friendships, stands as a testament to the enduring spirit of exploration that thrives within each of us, no matter our age. It reminds us that the greatest treasures are often found not on the well-trodden paths but in the detours we dare to take, where history, art, and human connection intertwine to create moments of unscripted beauty.

10.3 THE GREAT AMERICAN ROAD TRIP MIX-UP

In the dappled light of early morning, a senior couple, with maps spread out and a playlist of oldies but goodies queued up, anticipated the open road with a mix of excitement and a quiet sense of adventure. Their plan, meticulously plotted on a series of maps and apps, promised a journey through the heartland of America, replete with stops at landmarks both historic and scenic. Yet, as fate would have its playful hand in their departure, a mix-up in their route—swapped with another family's ambitious itinerary—set the stage for a series of detours that would color their travels with the unexpected.

Route Confusion

The initial realization that their path diverged from the familiar to the uncharted came not with frustration but a soft chuckle at the serendipity of it all. Highways once marked turned into byways unexplored as signs flashed by, heralding destinations outside their original plan. With each mile, the mix-up morphed from mishap to opportunity, the open road a canvas upon which their spontaneous adventure would be painted. Towns with names they'd never heard of beckoned with the promise of stories untold, each turn a question mark that begged exploration.

Scenic Misadventures

Their journey meandered, a winding river of asphalt that carried them through landscapes dotted with attractions of a peculiar charm. A giant ball of twine, its girth the result of years of dedication, offered a pause filled with wonder and bemusement. Roadside diners, each claiming the fame of the "best pie in the state," became culinary pit stops where tales from locals added layers to their travel tapestry. The lore of a ghost town whispered over cups of coffee piqued their curiosity, leading them down gravel roads to a place where history whispered back through the creak of old timbers and the sigh of the wind. Each detour, each unexpected stop, wove a narrative richer than any pre-planned itinerary could offer, their map a living document of their misadventures.

Navigational Nostalgia

As miles turned into memories, the couple found themselves adrift in reflections on the evolution of travel. Once mere points on a map, rest stops, and gas stations now stood as milestones marking time's passage, each visits a reminder of past road trips. They mused over the transformation of navigation from paper maps—creased and coffee-stained—to digital guides that chirped directions with sterile precision. Yet, amid modern convenience, they discovered a longing for the tactile connection of map to land, the joy of tracing a route with a fingertip, and the thrill of charting a course through unknown territories. With its blend of old and new, this journey became a bridge between the past and present, a celebration of the timeless spirit of exploration that roads, maps, and travelers share.

Journey's Joy

As their trip unfolded, the couple found themselves not just witnesses to the landscape but active participants in a larger story of discovery. The mix-up, once a source of mild concern, revealed itself as the heart of their adventure. This serendipitous guide led them to moments of beauty and connection. Laughter filled their car, a soundtrack that played over the engine's hum and the whisper of the wind. Conversations meandered like the roads they traveled, touching on dreams, the beauty of the unexpected, and the shared joy of adventure. In its twists and detours, they realized that the journey held the essence of their experience, a tapestry of moments that would be cherished long after the car was parked and the suitcases unpacked.

In this tapestry, each thread—the laughter shared over map mix-ups, the wonder at roadside curiosities, and the reflections on times past—wove together a narrative that celebrated the destinations and the journey itself. It was a reminder that life, much like their road trip, is enriched not by the certainty of plans but by the beauty found in detours, in the stories that unfold when the path diverges from the expected. As they looked forward to the miles yet to travel, they did so with a sense of openness to the road's call, ready to embrace the adventures that awaited, each mile a note in the melody of their journey.

In its meanderings and discoveries, this chapter mirrors our broader voyage, a journey marked by unexpected turns that challenge, delight, and ultimately shape our course. As we turn our gaze forward, let us carry with us the spirit of adventure, the warmth of shared laughter, and the wisdom found in the scenic routes of life.

CHAPTER 11

ECHOES OF LAUGHTER
IN THE DIGITAL AGE

I n a world where the threads of technology
and tradition intertwine, seniors often find
themselves at the crossroads of curiosity and
confusion. The advent of the selfie stick hailed as
a bridge between generations, serves as a beacon
of this intersection, illuminating the comedic
ballet of adaptation and the tender moments of
connection it fosters. With its extendable arm
and promise of capturing life from a new angle,
this tool becomes the catalyst for a series of explorations that are as fraught with error as they
are with discovery. Through the selfie stick saga
lens, we navigate the landscape of modern mar-
vels, where picture-perfect aspirations collide
with the reality of technological misadventures,

only to find that the true beauty lies in the shared laughter and the memories etched within these digital frames.

11.1 THE SELFIE STICK SAGA

A Modern Marvel

The acquisition of a selfie stick, much like the introduction of the rotary phone in its time, marks a significant moment in the digital odyssey of many seniors. Picture a sunny afternoon in a bustling park, where the air buzzes with families' laughter and birds chirping. Amidst this idyllic setting, a senior, armed with the newfound tool of a selfie stick, embarks on a quest to bridge the gap, to capture not just images but the essence of the moment. With its sleek design and button-pressed simplicity, the device holds the promise of inclusion, of selfies that encompass the whole family, pets included, without the acrobatics typically required to fit everyone into the frame.

Picture-Perfect Problems

Yet, as with all expeditions into unfamiliar territories, the path has pitfalls. The initial attempts at capturing the perfect selfie unfold like a comedy of errors. A picturesque scene by the lake, with the family gathered and smiles wide, is immortalized not with the click of a camera

but with the start of an accidental video, recording moments of confusion in place of poised perfection. Pets, ever the unpredictable elements in any family gathering, seize the moment to photobomb enthusiastically, turning serene shots into scenes of joyful chaos. The selfie stick, intended as a precision tool, becomes a wand of whimsy, orchestrating a dance of ducks and dives as the senior navigates its use.

Technological Teamwork

In this tango of technology, the younger members of the family step in, their expertise with digital devices as innate as breathing. This collaboration, unfolding in the shade of an old oak tree, is a symphony of instruction and experimentation. The grandchild, with a patience born of love, guides the senior through the steps, from adjusting the angle to capturing the light just right. The frustration that bubbles up is quickly dissolved in laughter, a shared acknowledgment of the learning curve that technology imposes. This intergenerational exchange, underpinned by a mutual desire to connect and capture memories, highlights the beauty of technological teamwork, where every misstep is a step towards greater understanding and closer bonds.

Captured Memories

In the end, the selfies captured, from the imperfectly perfect to the hilariously candid, become treasures, digital footprints of a day spent in the pursuit of connection. The selfie stick, once a symbol of the daunting bridge between generations, transforms into a totem of togetherness, a reminder of the laughter shared and the lessons learned. Each photo, a mosaic of faces and places, is a testament to seniors' resilience in navigating the digital age and their willingness to embrace new tools to hold moments close.

Visual Element: The Selfie Stick Journey

A photo collage, vibrant and sprawling, captures the essence of the selfie stick saga. Each image, framed by snippets of candid laughter and tender instruction, invites the viewer into the heart of the experience. Accompanying captions, penned in the handwriting of the participants, offer insights into the moments behind the photos, from the mishaps to the milestones. This visual diary, a patchwork of faces, places, and pets, is a testament to the journey undertaken, a narrative woven from the threads of technology, tradition, and the timeless pursuit of capturing life's fleeting moments.

Through the selfie stick saga, we navigate the nuances of adaptation, the trials accompanying the embrace of new technologies, and the triumphs found in the shared laughter and captured memories. This journey, marked by the interplay of confusion and discovery, underscores the enduring spirit of seniors as they chart their course through the digital age, guided by the light of curiosity and the warmth of familial bonds.

11.2 THE EMAIL THAT WAS MEANT TO BE A TEXT

In the quiet of early morning, when the world seems to hold its breath in anticipation of the day, a senior sits poised before the glow of a computer screen, fingers hesitantly hovering over the keyboard. This moment, ripe with the promise of connection, quickly spirals into a comedic tableau of digital misadventure. An urgent message, intended to swiftly leap across the digital divide via text, ensnared in the labyrinth of an email interface. The missive, laden with the immediacy of plans gone awry and the need for prompt redirection, languishes unnoticed in an inbox, its urgency diluted by the medium's formality. This digital faux pas, a mix-up emblematic of the ever-evolving communication technology landscape, sets the stage for an intergenerational dance of instruction, laughter, and eventual enlightenment.

The intervention comes in the form of a tech-savvy grandchild whose fluency in the digital dialect is as innate as breathing. Upon discovering the email's forlorn existence, this grandchild can't help but let loose a peal of laughter, a sound that dances through the room, light and unburdened by the weight of digital faux pas. The grandparents, initially bristled at the laughter, soon find themselves swept up in the humor of the situation. Together, they embark on a journey through the digital landscape, the grandchild serving as a guide, their instructions a gentle stream of knowledge that flows from their lips with ease and patience. This moment, ripe with potential frustration, transforms into a teachable one, laughter   bridging   the   chasm   of misunderstanding.

As the lesson unfolds, it becomes apparent that the divide between generations is not as vast as the technology that seems to widen it. The grand-parent, armed with newfound knowledge, ven-tures once more into the realm of digital communication, their following message success-fully finding its mark via text. However, victory is not without setbacks. Autocorrect, a well-meaning yet often misguided feature, takes liber-ties with their message, transforming a simple greeting into a nonsensical string of words and emojis. The recipient, another family member, receives this cryptic message with bemusement, sparking a series of exchanges that zigzag across platforms, from texts filled with unintended emojis to voice messages that capture the laughter and confusion of the moment.

Through these exchanges, a tapestry of commu-nication unfolds, each thread a testament to the myriad ways we connect in the digital age. Emails, with their formal veneer, offer space for thoughts to unfurl gracefully, while texts, swift and unencumbered by expectation, serve as snap-shots of moments and emotions. Voice messages, bridging the gap between text and call, carry with them the warmth of spoken words, a reminder of the human element that underpins all forms of communication. In this dance of digital dialogue, the senior finds not frustration but fascination, a newfound appreciation for the tools at their disposal.

This exploration of digital communication, sparked by a simple mix-up, blossoms into a celebration of connection in all its forms. Once wary of the pitfalls that lay in wait within the digital realm, the senior now navigates this landscape with a sense of adventure. They marvel at the ability to bridge distances with a click, to share laughter without delay, and to weave the fabric of their relationships tighter with each message, regardless of the medium. In this realm, where technology offers challenges and opportunities, the senior discovers the immutable truth underpinning our digital age: the importance of staying connected, no matter the platform.

The screen's glow softens as the day wanes, casting a gentle light on the senior's face. They sit, a figure poised between the analog past and the digital future, a bridge spanning generations. In their hands, the tools of communication—once sources of bewilderment—are now instruments of connection, wielded with a growing confidence. The laughter that once echoed through the room at the discovery of the email meant to be a text now resonates with a deeper timbre, a celebration of the journey from confusion to comprehension. In this quiet moment, as the boundary between the digital and the tangible blurs, the senior stands not at the periphery of the digital age but firmly within its embrace, connected across platforms, across generations, woven into the tapestry of the digital age with threads of laughter, learning, and an indomitable spirit of exploration.

11.3 THE ONLINE SHOPPING SPREE THAT WENT VIRAL

In an era where the digital realm burgeons with endless possibilities, a senior was inadvertently at the epicenter of a viral phenomenon, all thanks to a candid critique of a newly purchased gadget. This review, imbued with wit and unwitting humor, resonated with an audience far beyond the senior's modest social circle, catapulting them into the spotlight of internet acclaim. This unexpected twist in their online shopping journey highlighted their unique perspective on the array of modern products. It underscored the universal appeal of authenticity in a sea of polished endorsements.

Navigating through the virtual aisles of online shopping platforms became a newfound hobby, each click revealing a world brimming with gadgets and gizmos that promised to simplify life or add a dash of novelty to the mundane. The senior's exploration led to a collection of items as eclectic as they were intriguing, from kitchen appliances that boasted multifunctionality to wellness devices that melded ancient practices with contemporary technology. Each purchase was accompanied by a review, a narrative that vividly depicted the senior's adventures with the product. These critiques, peppered with anecdotes and light-hearted observations, transformed the mundane act of online shopping into an engaging saga that captivated readers and viewers alike.

The senior's rise to local fame was as rapid as unexpected. From being a casual shopper to becoming an "accidental influencer," their journey was marked by a growing audience that hung on their every word, eager for the following review or story. This newfound platform was more than just a medium for sharing purchase opinions. Still, it became a conduit for connecting with a diverse audience spanning generations and geographies. The candidness that characterized their reviews, from the triumphs of mastering a new smart device to the comedic pitfalls of assembling flat-packed furniture, struck a chord with many. This relatability, the unvarnished truth delivered with humor and grace, endeared the seniors to their followers, earning them a spot in the daily lives of people they had never met.

Amidst the whirlwind of likes, shares, and comments, a profound realization dawned upon the senior. The digital age, often criticized for its propensity to isolate, has woven a tapestry of vast, intimate connections. The online platform, a stage for their unexpected foray into the world of viral content, had become a virtual town square, a gathering place where laughter was shared, advice was sought, and stories were exchanged. Though born from the senior's shopping escapades and humorous misadventures, this community evolved into a space where dialogues unfolded, bridging the gap between the digital natives and those for whom technology was once an alien landscape.

The joy discovered in the digital age, encapsulated by the senior's viral shopping spree, was not confined to the products purchased or the fame acquired. It lay in the connections fostered, in the realization that the digital world was replete with opportunities for engagement, learning, and laughter. This journey, marked by clicks and carts, reviews and reactions, had transformed the senior from a solitary shopper into a beacon of light-hearted wisdom, a reminder that age is but a number in the vast digital expanse.

As the pixels of one adventure fade into the background, the anticipation for the next chapter swells. The narrative that began with a single viral review unfurls into a broader exploration of the intersections between seniors and the digital realm, a testament to the boundless potential for discovery, connection, and joy.

CHAPTER 12

SEASONS OF LAUGHTER

In the tapestry of life, humor stitches together the patches of joy and sorrow, creating a garment that warms the soul through the chill of autumn nights and the shadow play of flickering jack-o'-lanterns. Halloween, with its masquerade of ghouls and goblins, offers a canvas for creativity, a chance for every soul, young and old, to drape themselves in the fantastical, if only for a night. Within this spectral tableau, our tale unfurls, a narrative woven from the threads of imagination, misinterpretation, and the communal embrace of whimsy.

12.1 THE HALLOWEEN COSTUME THAT WON FIRST PRIZE...AND LAST PLACE

Creative Costumes

The challenge lay bare before them: conjuring a Halloween costume that would eclipse all others. This unique creation would become the stuff of legend. Inspiration struck in the guise of simplicity—a concept so obvious, it was overlooked, much like the last slice of pumpkin pie that everyone assumes someone else will enjoy. The idea was to embody the spirit of Halloween itself, not through the typical channels of vampires or witches, but through an abstract representation, a costume that was both everything and nothing, a true enigma.

Spooky Surprises

The unveiling was at the local community center, which had seen its fair share of pirates and princesses. Friends and family, their expectations set by years of traditional costumes, needed to prepare for the spectacle that awaited. The costume, an avant-garde amalgamation of

Halloween symbols—part jack-o'-lantern, part ghostly apparition, with a hint of scarecrow—defied categorization. Laughter erupted, not in derision but in delight at the sheer audacity of the concept. It was as if someone had decided to wear the essence of a brisk fall evening, which whispers tales of yore and mystery.

Award-Winning Antics

The judges, a panel accustomed to the conventional, found themselves at a crossroads. There was a costume that simultaneously captured the heart of Halloween and flouted every expectation. In a move as unexpected as the costume, they awarded it first prize for originality and last place for defying easy classification. This dual recognition became the talk of the town, a story retold with glee and a touch of awe. It was a testament to the event's spirit, where creativity was lauded and the lines between winning and losing blurred in the face of genuine ingenuity.

Festive Reflections

Much like the costume at its center, this tale serves as a reminder of the essential lightness of being that holidays, especially Halloween, bring to the fore. It underscores the importance of laughter, not taking oneself too seriously, and embracing the whimsical heart of festivities. Halloween, with its cloak of the supernatural, invites us to explore the boundaries of our imagination, to step beyond the veil of the mundane into a realm where laughter reigns supreme, a balm for the soul and a bridge between worlds.

Visual Element: The Enigma Unveiled

An infographic titled "The Enigma Unveiled" captures the essence of the costume and its reception. It breaks down the components of the outfit, each part annotated with humorous notes on the inspiration behind it and the reaction it garnered. Pie charts depict the judges' split decision. At the same time, a timeline tracks the costume's journey from concept to execution, interspersed with candid photos capturing the moment of revelation and the waves of laughter that followed. This visual compendium serves as a memento of the occasion and an invitation to reflect on the joy that creativity and a dash of daring can bring to our lives.

12.2 THE CHRISTMAS LIGHTS THAT TANGLED UP THE TOWN

In a quaint corner of the world where snowflakes danced like wayward stars and the crisp air whispered of impending festivities, a plan germinated within the heart of the community. This wasn't just any scheme but an audacious dream to drape the town in a cloak of lights so resplendent it would beckon the holiday spirit from the far reaches of the earth. The endeavor was colossal, a symphony of illumination that promised to paint the night in hues of joy and wonder. Yet, as with all things grand, the path was strewn with unexpected hurdles, the first of which was a labyrinth of tangled lights that seemed almost sentient in their refusal to unknot.

The town square, traditionally a serene space that echoed the footsteps of its residents, transformed into a battleground where strands of lights waged war against the well-meaning townsfolk. Armed with patience and an unwavering resolve, volunteers gathered under the banner of communal spirit, each tug at the knotted mess a testament to their dedication. Laughter, that universal solvent, permeated the air, diffusing tension and knitting the volunteers closer with every pull and twist. It was a sight to behold, a tableau of unity and perseverance set against the backdrop of a town cloaked in the anticipation of Christmas.

As dusk blanketed the sky, casting long shadows that danced alongside the volunteers, a breakthrough shimmered on the horizon. Once a tangled web of defiance, the lights lay sorted and ready to adorn the lampposts, trees, and eaves that marked the town's landscape. The task, Herculean in its essence, had fostered an environment where every individual, regardless of age or prowess, contributed to the tapestry of light that would soon envelop the town. The switch-on ceremony, anticipated with bated breath, was not merely a formality but a crescendo of collective achievement, a moment where every heart in attendance beat in synchrony with the flicker of the bulbs.

And then, with a flick and a whisper of hope, the town erupted in a spectacle of light that rivaled the stars above. The display, a cascade of twinkling wonders, bathed the city in a glow that spoke of magic and dreams woven from the fabric of the holiday spirit. Faces, young and old, reflected the myriad lights, their expressions a mixture of awe and pride. Children danced in the streets, their laughter mingling with the melodies of carols that floated through the air, an anthem to the joy and warmth the season heralds.

Yet, it was not the flawless execution of the light display that would linger in the memories of those present but the journey that led to its creation. The mishaps and hurdles, the tangled wires and knotted bulbs had unwittingly woven a more robust fabric of the community, imbuing the festive season with a deeper meaning. The lights, in their luminescent splendor, were but stars in a larger constellation of experiences that defined the town's foray into the holiday season. They were reminders of the chaos that precedes beauty, the laughter that echoes through moments of frustration, and the unity that emerges from shared endeavors.

The square thrummed with life as the night deepened, casting the town in a glow that seemed to hold back the darkness. Stories of the day's escapades were shared over steaming cups of cocoa, each a thread in the rich tapestry of community life. In their silent vigil, the lights stood as beacons of a holiday spirit rekindled not just by the desire for beauty but by the warmth of togetherness.

In this corner of the world, where the night was alight with its inhabitants' dreams, the holiday spirit's true essence was redefined. It was found not in the perfection of the light display but in the imperfections that marked its creation, in the laughter that rose like a phoenix from the ashes of frustration, and in the memories that would glow long after the last light was extinguished. The Christmas lights that tangled up the town had, in their intricate dance of confusion and beauty, illuminated more than just the physical space; they had lit the way to understanding that the most profound holiday moments are birthed from the unexpected, from the shared laughter and collective sighs of a community united in its pursuit of light.

12.3 THE EASTER EGG HUNT WITH A SURPRISE VISITOR

In the heart of spring, when the air is suffused with the scent of blooming flowers and the earth itself seems to hum with new life, a community gathered to weave a tapestry of tradition and joy through an Easter egg hunt. This event envisioned as a labyrinth of hidden treasures and playful challenges, promised to infuse the season with bursts of color and laughter, a celebration designed to beckon both the young and young at heart into the embrace of communal gaiety. Orchestrators of this annual rite plotted the placement of eggs with the precision of cartographers, each location chosen not only for its ability to conceal but also to surprise, weaving a narrative of discovery that would unfold beneath the tender gaze of the spring sun.

As dawn broke on the day of the hunt, a curious visitor, drawn by the kaleidoscope of colors and the whisper of festivities on the breeze, ventured into the heart of the celebration. This guest, a young deer with eyes wide and wonder moved with tentative steps, its presence a silent testament to the allure of the community's preparations. The initial encounters, marked by startled gasps and delighted chuckles, quickly transformed from moments of surprise to opportunities for enchantment. With its gentle demeanor and unbridled curiosity, the deer became not an intruder but a participant, a bridge between the wildness of nature and the crafted joy of the hunt.

Adaptation, that ever-present undercurrent in the flow of life, stirred within the hearts of the organizers and attendees. Initially charted as a course for human feet, the hunt expanded its embrace to include this unexpected guest, turning the day into an even richer tapestry of interaction and mirth. Children, their baskets swinging from eager hands, paused in their quest for confectionary treasures to marvel at the deer, its presence an unexpected gift that no egg could rival. Laughter rippled through the air, a melody harmonized with the soft rustle of grass beneath delicate hooves, as the community found joy not only in the hunt but in the shared experience of wonder and coexistence.

The culmination of the day's festivities, marked not by the tally of eggs gathered but by the wealth of memories woven, reflected the season's essence. Spring, with its narrative of renewal and growth, found a parallel in the community's embrace of the unexpected, in the willingness to incorporate the serendipity of a deer's visit into the fabric of their celebration. The realization that the best-laid plans often give way to the most delightful surprises became the day's greatest lesson, a reminder that joy usually resides in the spontaneous and the unplanned.

As the shadows lengthened and the last rays of the sun dipped below the horizon, painting the sky with strokes of pink and gold, the community gathered once more. This assembly, a mosaic of individuals united by the day's shared experiences, stood as a testament to the enduring allure of communal festivities and the bonds they forge. The laughter that had punctuated the day, born from the interplay of anticipation and surprise, echoed in the soft evening air. This chorus spoke of the ties that bind us to each other and the natural world.

In this celebration of spring and renewal, the community discovered that the true treasures of the season lie not beneath the sheltering embrace of foliage or within the colorful shells of hidden eggs but in the moments of connection and joy shared among friends, family, and the unexpected guests that life brings into our circle. The Easter egg hunt, with its surprise visitor and the adaptability it inspired, wove a narrative of community, laughter, and embracing life's unforeseen gifts. This story mirrors the broader journey of life itself.

As we close this chapter, we carry forward the memories of laughter shared in the glow of spring, traditions upheld and adapted, and the community that grows stronger with each shared experience. These stories, rich with the hues of life and the warmth of togetherness, pave the way for the tales yet to be told, for the chapters yet to unfold in the grand narrative of our shared journey.

CHAPTER 13

WHISPERS AND ECHOES FROM THE FEATHERED FRIENDS

In the quiet of dawn, when the world seems to hold its breath in anticipation of the day, a peculiar symphony unfolds in the heart of a small town. This melody, woven from the whispers of nature, becomes the backdrop for a tale of connection and laughter that transcends the boundaries between species. It's here, under the canopy of a waking sky, that we find a narrative not of grand adventures but of the profound joy in the simplicity of daily interactions with the avian inhabitants of our world.

13.1 THE LADY WHO TALKED TO BIRDS

A Special Bond

Imagine a garden where the morning light filters through the leaves, casting dappled shadows on the dew-kissed grass. In this serene setting, a woman stands, her presence a familiar fixture to the feathered denizens that flock to her side. Like clockwork, her voice rises in a gentle cadence each morning, a greeting to the day and its winged witnesses. This ritual, unnoticed by most, becomes a spectacle for those who pause long enough to observe—the birds, responding in their chirps and trills, engage in what appears to be a dialogue with their human counterpart. Initially perplexed by this exchange, neighbors soon find themselves drawn to the fence that borders the garden, their curiosity piqued by the uncommon sight of a human seemingly conversing with birds.

Feathered Messengers

As seasons cycle from the bloom of spring to the whisper of autumn leaves, the woman's interactions with the birds evolve into a source of local lore. Observations lead to the realization that her feathered friends, through their arrival patterns and the urgency of their calls, seem to forecast the weather with surprising accuracy. A flurry of activity and agitated song predicts a storm on the horizon. At the same time, a serene gathering under the morning sun foretells a day of clear skies. This uncanny correlation between the birds' behavior and the weather earns the woman a reputation as a local oracle, her predictions sought after by gardeners and planners of outdoor events alike.

The Bird Choir

An annual neighborhood meeting, traditionally a solemn affair focused on budgets and by-laws, becomes the stage for an unexpected performance. Mid-discussion, a chorus of birdcalls fills the air, a serenade orchestrated by the woman from her garden nearby. The meeting, momentarily derailed, succumbs to the charm of this impromptu concert. Laughter replaces the furrowed brows of deliberation; the woman's feathered choir reminds the attendees of the lighter side of life. This interruption, far from being a nuisance, becomes a highlight of the meeting, a story retold with fondness in the following years.

Legacy of Laughter

The woman's presence in the neighborhood, marked by her daily dialogues with the birds, fosters a sense of unity and joy among its inhabitants. Once a private sanctuary, her garden becomes a symbol of community. In this place, nature's melodies remind everyone of the importance of pausing, listening, and finding harmony in our surroundings. The birds, no longer just background music to the rush of daily life, stand as messengers of laughter and lightness, their interactions with the woman a testament to the unexpected connections that enrich our lives.

Interactive Element: Birdsong Diary

Keeping a birdsong diary encourages readers to tune into the natural world outside their windows. This activity involves recording the times of day when certain birds are heard, noting weather conditions, and observing any correlations between bird activity and environmental changes. It's a practice that fosters mindfulness and a deeper appreciation for the rhythms of nature.

Through the lens of the lady who talked to birds, we're reminded that joy often resides in the quiet moments of connection with the natural world. Her story, a blend of whimsy and wisdom, invites us to listen more closely to the world around us, find the extraordinary in the ordinary, and embrace the laughter and lessons our feathered friends offer.

13.2 THE MAN WHO INVENTED A NEW HOLIDAY

Innovation in Celebration

In a quaint neighborhood, where the rhythm of daily life hummed with comforting predictability, a spark of ingenuity flickered within the mind of an unassuming resident. This individual, known among his peers for a penchant for whimsy and a heart brimming with benevolence, gazed upon the calendar with a playful discontent. Amidst the mosaic of dates commemorating grand historical events and venerable figures, he perceived a void —an absence of a day dedicated to the unsung heroes who colored the fabric of everyday existence with their quiet dedication. Stirred by this realization, he conceived of a novel festivity, a holiday unmarked on any official register but profound in its intent. This celebration would not herald the deeds of the illustrious. Still, it would shine a light on those whose contributions, though often overlooked, were the threads holding together the tapestry of community life.

Community Festivities

The genesis of this holiday was modest, its observance confined to the boundaries of a neighborhood yet to grasp the magnitude of the tradition it was birthing. The inaugural event was a pancake breakfast, held at dawn in the local park, a feast in honor of the postal workers whose daily rounds were the lifelines of communication. Tables laden with syrupy stacks and steaming mugs became altars of appreciation, around which gathered a congregation united in gratitude. As the sun climbed higher, the festivities morphed, taking on a vibrant life of their own. A parade ensued, not of floats and fanfare, but of pets and their human companions—a motley procession celebrating the bond between species, each pet adorned in attire befitting their role as the unsung comforters of lonely hearts. The day unfolded like a tapestry of joy, each event a stitch in the vibrant quilt of community celebration, from the serenade for the street sweepers to the twilight toast for the teachers who nurtured the minds of the young.

Viral Holiday

What began as a spark in the heart of one man soon kindled a blaze that spread beyond the confines of his neighborhood, its warmth touching communities distant and diverse. The holiday, nurtured in the cradle of a tiny town, found resonance in the universal human longing for connection and recognition. Social media became the wind that carried this ember of innovation to far-flung corners, where it ignited celebrations of a similar spirit. Towns adopted unique observances, each tailored to the local tapestry of unsung heroes, from the librarians who guarded the bastions of knowledge to the bus drivers who charted the daily odysseys of commuters. The holiday transcended its origins, morphing into a mosaic of local traditions, each community adding its hue to the spectrum of celebration. Recognition came, unbidden yet deserved, from sources as varied as city councils to national broadcasters, each acknowledging the power of a day dedicated to the extraordinary within the ordinary.

The Power of Appreciation

As the holiday wove its way into the fabric of broader society, it brought into sharp relief the profound impact of appreciation on the human spirit. This festivity, rooted in the whimsical notion of one individual, blossomed into a testament to the transformative power of gratitude. It served as a mirror, reflecting the myriad ways the ordinary heroes among us shaped the quality of our daily lives, often without fanfare or expectation of reward. The celebration became a conduit for the expression of thanks, a collective acknowledgment that the essence of a community's strength lay not in the grandeur of its achievements but in the sum of its small kindnesses. It underscored the notion that heroism was not the sole province of the extraordinary. Still, it was woven through the actions of the every day, through every smile offered in consolation, every hand extended in assistance, and every act of kindness rendered without thought of recompense.

In this unveiling of a new holiday, the tapestry of human experience was enriched, imbued with a deeper appreciation for the myriad roles played by each community member. It underscored the beauty inherent in the act of recognition, revealing that within the heart of gratitude lay the seeds of a joy vast and boundless. This celebration, conceived in the mind of one but embraced by many, stood as a beacon of the enduring power of acknowledgment, a reminder that in celebrating the unsung, we weave a narrative of community that elevates the mundane to the magnificent.

13.3 THE DOG THAT BECAME MAYOR FOR A DAY

In the tapestry of a small town's life, where every thread weaves a story of community and camaraderie, a peculiar election stirred the winds of change and laughter. This wasn't an ordinary electoral battle with promises and policies but a heartwarming nomination of a four-legged friend known to all as the community dog. His name was whispered from corner to corner with a fondness usually reserved for local heroes. His campaign, if one could call it that, was laced with neither agendas nor ambitions but a simple, unspoken consensus to uplift spirits while supporting a noble cause—animal welfare.

The dog's ascension to the honorary title of mayor for a day was met with unanimous joy, not just for the novelty it presented but for the unity it symbolized. It was an acknowledgment that sometimes, leadership could be measured in tail wags and friendly barks. His inaugural day dawned with a series of engagements that would see him cutting ribbons with a paw shake at newly inaugurated dog parks, his presence a seal of approval for spaces that promised freedom and joy for his kind. But his duties extended beyond the ceremonial. He presided over a pet adoption fair, where his gentle nudge and approving sniff seemed to seal the fate of many a lonely pet in search of a home. The sight of the canine mayor, adorned with a sash that humorously declared his office, moving from one engagement to another, brought smiles and laughter, a reminder of the simple joys that bind a community.

Yet, his tenure, though brief, still needed its edicts. With a playful glint in his eyes, he issued his first decree—naptime was henceforth a civic duty, a period of rest sanctified by stretches and yawns, to be observed by all, regardless of species. His second, a mandate for mandatory belly rubs, was met with enthusiastic compliance, transforming public spaces into arenas of affection and connection. These whimsical policies, issued from the heart of a dog who knew no malice, were received with the warmth they were intended, each "law" an invitation to pause, to revel in the moment, and to appreciate the bonds that connect us all.

As the sun dipped below the horizon, marking the end of his mayoralty, the legacy of his tenure was already taking shape—not in statutes or edicts but in the laughter and love he inspired. The day served not just as a celebration of his spirit but as a collective reflection on the roles animals play in our lives, as companions, teachers of unconditional love, and as reminders of the joy found in simplicity. The funds raised during his term, a substantial sum destined for local animal shelters, stood as a testament to the generosity of a community united by a dog's whimsical yet profound leadership.

While fleeting, the canine mayor's day in office left an indelible mark on the town, a chapter in its history where humor and goodwill triumphed, illustrating the power of unity in pursuit of a common good. It was a day when laughter filled the air, hearts swelled with pride, and the often-overlooked plight of animal welfare found a spotlight. His mayoralty, though symbolic, underscored a more profound truth—that leadership is not confined to the bipedal, that wisdom can be found in the unlikeliest of mayors, and that sometimes, the best way to lead is simply by being one's authentic self.

As the moon rises to take its place among the stars, casting a soft glow over a town still buzzing with the day's joy, we are gently reminded that the essence of the community lies not in grand gestures but in the shared moments of happiness and the collective embrace of whimsical endeavors. In his innocence and exuberance, the dog who became mayor for a day taught us that leadership can be as simple as leading with one's heart and that even the smallest paw can leave an enduring imprint on the fabric of our lives.

In this narrative, where tails wag in approval and laughter rings clear, we glimpse the beauty of life's more superficial aspects. This beauty connects us across boundaries and species. It reminds us that in the heart of every community, there beats a rhythm of unity, a rhythm that dances to the tune of shared joy and collective goodwill.

CHAPTER 14

MISCHIEF IN THE MIX: THE ALCHEMY OF ACCIDENTS

I n the heart of a bustling community kitchen, where the aroma of baking dough and simmering spices mingle, an event unfolded that would forever alter the culinary landscape of a small town. This wasn't just any gathering; it was the annual pie baking contest, a revered tradition where local bakers, from the seasoned to the novice, showcased their prowess, vying for the coveted title of Pie Champion. Yet, this year's contest was destined to diverge from its well-trodden path, veering into uncharted territory, thanks to a culinary curveball that none saw coming.

14.1 THE PIE BAKING CONTEST WITH AN UNEXPECTED INGREDIENT

A Culinary Curveball

The day dawned bright and clear. The kitchen buzzed with anticipation; aprons were tied, and ovens were preheated. Amidst the flurry of activity, a simple mix-up in the pantry set the stage for an unprecedented twist. Flour, the backbone of pie crusts, was inadvertently swapped with powdered sugar, a mistake unnoticed in the heat of competition. Aspies emerged from ovens, their golden crusts hiding the sweet secret within; bakers beamed with pride, unaware of the surprise that awaited.

Taste Test Turmoil

The judges, a panel comprising the town's most esteemed culinary figures, approached their task with the gravitas it deserved. The first bite, however, sent eyebrows arching in surprise. The expected savory succulence of a classic meat pie was usurped by an unexpected sweetness, throwing taste buds into disarray. Each subsequent pie presented a disconcerting blend of flavors, from the tangy embrace of a lemon meringue to the robust earthiness of a mushroom and thyme creation. The kitchen, once a bastion of focused activity, erupted in a cacophony of confusion and laughter as the source of the anomaly came to light.

Community Creativity

What could have been a disaster transformed into a celebration of culinary creativity? Rather than adjudicating traditional pies, the contest became an impromptu innovation showcase. Bakers, embracing the spirit of the moment, pitched their creations with a twist, marketing their pies as avant-garde interpretations of classic recipes. The community, drawn by the unusual turn of events, rallied around the bakers, sampling the array of pies with open minds and adventurous palates. This unexpected ingredient sparked a tradition of experimentation, encouraging bakers in subsequent contests to explore and infuse their pies with unconventional elements, expanding the boundaries of pie-making.

The Sweet Taste of Innovation

Reflections on the day underscored a broader truth; within the realm of accidents lies the potential for discovery. The simple error mix-up catalyzed a shift in perspective, illustrating how the unexpected can serve as a conduit for growth and innovation. It echoed the sentiments in every culinary experiment's heart: the courage to embrace the unknown and the joy of unearthing new possibilities. Once a showcase of technical skill, the contest evolved into a testament to the adaptive spirit of the community, a celebration of the alchemy that occurs when accidents collide with creativity.

Interactive Element: Pie Innovation Challenge

A call to action for readers, the Pie Innovation Challenge encourages them to venture into their kitchens and experiment with unconventional ingredients, pushing the boundaries of traditional pie recipes. Participants are invited to document their process, from selecting their surprise ingredient to the final, taste-tested creation, sharing their experiences and recipes with the community through a dedicated online platform. This interactive element not only fosters a sense of connection among readers but also celebrates the spirit of culinary exploration, underscoring the belief that new flavors, textures, and traditions can arise from the unexpected.

In this chapter, where flour clouds settled and laughter echoed off tiled walls, the story of the pie-baking contest unfolded—a narrative not of competition but of camaraderie, not of perfection but of exploration. It served as a reminder that within the crucible of the kitchen, as in life, the most memorable moments often arise from the unforeseen, weaving together the ingredients of creativity, community, and the sweet taste of innovation.

14.2 THE COMMUNITY PLAY WITH TOO MANY DIRECTORS

In the embrace of an evening that held the promise of theatrical magic, the local community hall morphed into a vibrant arena of artistic expression. Here, amidst the scent of fresh paint on makeshift backdrops and the soft rustle of costumes hurriedly donned, a narrative of unparalleled creativity and chaos was about to unfold.

Traditionally a harmonious endeavor, this year's community play found itself in the clutches of a well-intentioned yet ultimately tumultuous decision: to appoint not one but several directors, each harboring visions as diverse as the hues of a sunset.

Dramatic Directives

The rehearsal space, a crucible of artistic ambition, became a battleground for conflicting script interpretations. One director envisioned a setting steeped in the stark minimalism of modern theater. At the same time, another sought to drape the production in the rich tapestries of historical accuracy. Yet another director, enamored by the potential of abstract expressionism, proposed a stage devoid of all but the most symbolic of props. Actors found themselves adrift in a sea of directives, each wave of instruction clashing with the next, creating a patchwork quilt of performance styles that threatened to unravel at the seams. It was within this maelstrom of creativity that the essence of the play began to metamorphose, taking on a life of its own, untethered from the original script.

Stage Shenanigans

As the curtain rose, the actors, now seasoned navigators of this tumultuous sea, embraced the unpredictability of their situation. Once a meticulously planned affair, costume changes evolved into impromptu decisions made in the shadows of the wings, guided by the flickering intuition of the cast. Lines, memorized under the tutelage of differing artistic philosophies, melded into a tapestry of ad-libbed dialogue that danced between the intended narrative and spontaneous bursts of creativity. The crew, once the silent sentinels of order, became co-conspirators in this artistic rebellion, their cues morphing to match the fluidity of the performance. It was a spectacle of improvisation, a testament to the adaptability and ingenuity of those thrust into the whirlwind of too many directors.

A Performance to Remember

The audience, an unsuspecting congregation of community members, found themselves on a voyage through uncharted theatrical waters. Laughter erupted in waves, a chorus of delight and bewilderment that ebbed and flowed with the tide of the performance. Scenes intended to tug at the heartstrings transformed into comedic interludes. At the same time, moments designed for laughter took on a poignant depth, reflective of the serendipitous beauty found amidst chaos. The final act, a crescendo of confusion and clarity, culminated in a standing ovation that thundered through the hall, acknowledging the journey shared by performers and spectators alike. It was a performance etched into the community's collective memory, a vibrant mosaic of what occurs when artistic visions collide and coalesce in the most unexpected ways.

Unity in Variety

In the aftermath of the curtain's fall, a profound realization took root as actors and directors gathered amidst the remnants of their shared endeavor. The diversity of vision, rather than diluting the essence of the play, had enriched it, weaving a tapestry of creativity that resonated with the multifaceted nature of the human experience. This experiment in artistic governance, though chaotic, underscored the beauty inherent in collaboration, in the melding of disparate ideas into a unified whole. It was a celebration of the community's capacity for creativity, demonstrating how the confluence of differing perspectives can give rise to experiences that transcend the ordinary, crafting moments of unexpected joy and unity from the fabric of diversity.

In this narrative of a community play transformed by the multitude of its directors, we find not just a story of artistic endeavor but a reflection on the broader tapestry of life itself. It reminds us that within the cacophony of conflicting ideas and visions lies the potential for harmony, for the creation of something truly extraordinary. This tale, woven from the threads of ambition, creativity, and collective spirit, serves as a beacon for all who seek to navigate the complexities of collaboration, offering a glimpse into the magic that unfolds when we embrace the beautiful chaos of diversity in pursuit of a common goal.

14.3 THE YARD SALE THAT BECAME A BLOCK PARTY

In the dawn's soft glow, a quiet street awakened to the clatter of relics from attics and the back of closets finding their way onto lawns and driveways. This was no ordinary Saturday morning, the day of the neighborhood yard sale, an event marked on calendars with a blend of anticipation and nostalgia. Yet, as tables laden with the tapestry of past decades began to line the sidewalks, an unscripted transformation took root, turning a simple sale into a vibrant block party.

The initial intent was clear: to declutter, to part with the unused and the outgrown. However, as neighbors sauntered from lawn to lawn, the air became thick with stories and laughter, the currency of exchange as valuable as the cash changing hands. One person's forgotten vinyl collection became another's treasure, a bridge across generations built on the grooves of a record. Children, eyes wide with wonder, discovered toys their parents once cherished. At the same time, kitchen gadgets of dubious utility found new homes, their purposes debated with humor and inventiveness.

Amidst the bargaining and banter, grills were fired up, and picnic tables became laden with an impromptu feast. What had begun as individual sales merged into a communal celebration, with each household contributing to the spread. Music drifted through the air, a soundtrack to the day's festivities, as people found themselves not just haggling over prices but sharing recipes, gardening tips, and life stories. In its evolution, the yard sale became a canvas upon which the neighborhood painted a picture of unity and joyous communal living.

The true magic of the day was found in the unexpected treasures, those items that elicited gasps of recognition or peals of laughter. A vintage lamp, its shade slightly askew, sparked a conversation about design trends of decades past, its soft light illuminating the faces of those gathered around. A collection of old postcards, sent from corners of the world now changed by time, offered glimpses into journeys long before GPS and smartphones, inspiring tales of adventure and wonder. And amid it all, a peculiar gadget of indeterminate purpose became the show's star, its function debated with a mix of curiosity and amusement, a reminder of the whimsy in the unknown.

As the sun descended, casting long shadows that danced on the pavement, the street hummed with warmth beyond the day's physical heat. This gathering had transcended the mere act of buying and selling, morphing into a celebration of community and connection. Neighbors, some of whom had only exchanged polite nods over the years, found themselves laughing together, sharing stories and food, their lives intertwining in the shared space of their street. In its serendipitous evolution into a block party, the yard sale wove a more robust fabric of neighborliness, a tapestry rich with the threads of newfound friendships and kindred spirits.

The day offered a profound reflection on the essence of community in this symphony of exchanges, both material and emotional. It underscored the beauty found in the simplicity of coming together, turning a transactional moment into an opportunity for connection. The items that changed hands were more than just possessions; they were stories, memories, and bridges between past and present, catalysts for conversations that might never have occurred otherwise. This event, marked by laughter and the clinking of glasses, by the sharing of meals and memories, was a vivid illustration of how the most rewarding gatherings are often those that blossom spontaneously, nurtured by the collective spirit of a community.

As the remnants of the day were packed away, the street quiet once more, an air of contentment lingered, a sense of fulfillment that extended beyond the successful sales. The yard sale that became a block party stood as a testament to the transformative power of community, the joy that arises from shared experiences, and the strength in the bonds of neighborliness. It was a reminder that in the heart of every neighborhood lies the potential for moments of unexpected delight and connection, waiting to be unearthed like treasures at a yard sale.

As we reflect on this day and turn the pages of our collective story, we find a simple truth woven into the fabric of our being: that the essence of life's richness lies not in the accumulation of things but in the connections we forge, in the laughter we share, and in the communal spirit that thrives in the unscripted moments of togetherness.

CHAPTER 15

UNLIKELY PATHWAYS TO CONNECTION

I n the labyrinth of life's encounters, the most unassuming interactions often lead to the richest tapestries of connection. Picture this: a bustling coffee shop on a rain-drenched Tuesday morning, where a spilled latte catalyzes an unlikely friendship. Within such unforeseen moments, life's true serendipities are unveiled, revealing the profound impact of openness to the world and its myriad inhabitants.

15.1 THE STRANGER WHO BECAME A FRIEND

An Unexpected Meeting

On a nondescript Wednesday, two individuals found themselves side by side at a local bus stop, sheltering from an unexpected downpour. The first, a retiree with a penchant for bird watching, clutching a weather-beaten field guide; the second, a young professional, eyes glued to the relentless scroll of a smartphone. The silence between them, initially as dense as the storm clouds overhead, was soon broken by a shared challenge: deciphering the bus schedule, rendered nearly illegible by the rain's assault. Through shared laughter at the absurdity of their predicament and a mutual appreciation for the rain's unexpected beauty, a bridge was built over the chasm of their initial differences.

Common Ground

As the wait lengthened, an exchange of stories unfolded, weaving from the mundane to the profound. The retiree spoke of mornings spent in the company of sparrows and finches, of the quiet joy found in their simple existence. The younger listener shared tales of digital landscapes navigated, of connections made and lost within the ether of the internet. Surprisingly, a common thread emerged: a shared fascination with the narratives that shape our lives, whether sung from the boughs of a tree or typed with thumbs on a glowing screen. This revelation, that at the heart of their experiences lay a mutual quest for connection, deepened the bond that the rain had begun to forge.

A Friendship Forms

In the following weeks, what began as chance encounters at the bus stop evolved into deliberate meetings, the bus stop becoming their chosen rendezvous. Conversations meandered through topics as varied as the migratory patterns of birds and the latest trends in social media, each offering the other a window into their world. Small acts of kindness—a shared umbrella, a cup of coffee bought in secret and provided with a smile —cemented their burgeoning friendship. This evolution from strangers to confidantes under-scored a simple truth: the potential for profound connection lies within each shared moment, no matter how mundane.

The Value of Openness

Reflecting on the unfolding of this friendship, it becomes clear that its foundation was built not on shared history or common interests but on a willingness to engage with the unknown. It serves as a reminder that openness to the people who cross our paths, the stories they carry, and the experiences they offer can transform the fabric of our daily lives. Like a garden where di-verse species flourish side by side, drawing strength from their differences, so too can our lives be enriched by the unexpected friendships that bloom in the most unlikely of soils.

Visual Element: The Intersection of Worlds

A series of candid photographs captures the essence of this evolving friendship. The first photo is a snapshot of two figures under a shared umbrella, their laughter barely contained by the frame. The next is a close-up of hands exchanging a field guide and a smartphone, symbolic of their exchange of worlds. The final photo is a candid shot of shared coffee at their now-favorite café, where laughter and conversation flow as freely as the rain outside. Accompanying these images, a journal prompt invites readers to reflect on their encounters with strangers, encouraging them to explore the potential for connection in everyday interactions.

The story of two individuals at a rain-soaked bus stop explores unlikely pathways to connection and is a testament to the power of openness. It reminds us that the journey to friendship often begins with a single step outside our comfort zone into the embrace of the unknown. As we navigate the intricate web of human interaction, let us carry with us the bus stop's lesson: within every unexpected meeting lies the seed of a potential friendship, waiting only for the nurturing light of our openness to bring it into bloom.

15.2 THE LOST KITTEN THAT FOUND A HOME

A Furry Discovery

In the dappled shade of a community garden, where the chatter of neighbors mingled with the rustle of leaves, a soft mewling disturbed the afternoon's tranquility. Nestled among the roots of an old oak tree, a small, forlorn figure trembled, its fur matted and eyes wide with uncertainty. This kitten, barely a whisper of life amid the verdant sprawl of vegetables and flowers, ignited a spark of concern that quickly flared into a collective endeavor. Word of the discovery rippled through the neighborhood, drawing a crowd that, only moments before, had been absorbed in their separate lives. The garden, a place of individual toil and joy, transformed into a stage for a shared mission, the plight of the lost kitten weaving a thread of purpose through the heartstrings of the community.

Collective Care

As the sun dipped lower, casting amber hues over the garden, a plan emerged from the assembly of concerned neighbors. Materials for a makeshift shelter appeared as if by magic, cobbled together from garden sheds and generous homes. A soft bed was fashioned from old sweaters, and bowls of water and milk were placed with hopeful anticipation. Once a quivering bundle of fear, the kitten began to explore its temporary haven with tentative steps, encouraged by the gentle words and patient presence of its newfound guardians. A schedule materialized as a testament to the community's determination, each slot filled with the names of those committed to the kitten's care. Nightly vigils were held, stories shared under the whispering leaves, and caring for the vulnerable creature drew the neighbors into a circle of light and warmth. This collective vigil, marked by shared laughter and soft lullabies, sowed the seeds of camaraderie in the fertile ground of empathy, each feeding and cuddling session a stitch in the ever-expanding fabric of community connection.

A Happy Resolution

Days passed, and with each sunrise, the kitten grew more robust, its playful antics a source of delight for its rotating cadre of caretakers. Posters and online pleas had yielded no claimants to the tiny wanderer, and the question of its future began to loom large in discussions. During one such gathering, as the kitten dozed in the lap of its latest guardian, a decision was reached—not with fanfare, but with a quiet certainty that spoke of deep bonds forged in unexpected circumstances. The family, long-time residents, and avid community garden supporters offered to give the kitten a permanent home; their gesture met with nods of approval and misty eyes. The adoption ceremony, simple yet imbued with significance, took place beneath the oak tree that had first cradled the lost soul, the garden bearing witness to the moment the kitten's journey came full circle. This creature, once an emblem of vulnerability, became a symbol of the neighborhood's capacity for love and action, a living reminder of the strength inherent in unity and the transformative power of collective care.

The Bonds That Bind

In the following weeks, the kitten—now a vibrant and curious explorer of its new domain—played a central role in the neighborhood's tapestry. Its presence at garden gatherings, often perched regally atop a pile of cushions or darting among the rows of plants, served as a visual testament to the journey undertaken by the community. Conversations, once limited to polite exchanges about the weather or the yield of tomato plants, deepened into discussions about responsibility and how to care for the least among us can mirror our shared humanity. The act of saving one tiny, scared kitten had, in essence, rescued a community from the confines of individualism, weaving them into a collective defined by compassion and action. This subtle yet profound transformation underscored a fundamental truth: by extending our hearts and hands to others, whether human or animal, we provide sanctuary for those in need and fortify the bonds that anchor us to one another. Through this shared endeavor, a neighborhood found a new mascot and a renewed sense of identity, one rooted in the understanding that our capacity to care, to come together in moments of need, is perhaps the most defining—and endearing—aspect of the human experience.

15.3 THE BENCH BY THE LAKE WITH A STORY TO TELL

Nestled on the verdant banks of a tranquil lake, a solitary bench stands, its wooden slats weathered by the seasons, bearing silent witness to the ebb and flow of countless lives. This bench, unremarkable at first glance, has evolved into a revered haven within the community. In this place, solace, inspiration, and companionship are discovered amidst the gentle lapping of water against the shore. Etched into its very grain are the echoes of laughter, the whispers of confessions, and the silent tears of solitary contemplation, each marking the bench as a custodian of human experience.

In the dawning light, when the mist still clings to the lake's surface, the elderly come to bask in the serene beginnings of the day, their presence a quiet ode to the enduring beauty of nature. Here, they find a respite from the relentless march of time, a momentary pause in which the world does not demand but simply offers its subtle wonders for appreciation. The bench becomes a classroom where lessons are not taught but felt, wisdom imparted through the simple act of being present within the natural world.

As the sun climbs higher, the bench witnesses the tentative steps of new friendships forming in its shadow. A shared glance, a laugh over a shared story; these are the moments when connections are forged, not through grand gestures but through the quiet acknowledgment of shared humanity. A young mother finds solace in the understanding smile of another, their conversations weaving the common threads of their lives into a tapestry of mutual understanding and support. Here, on this unassuming bench, barriers dissolve, allowing for genuine interaction unencumbered by the walls people so often build around themselves.

Through the years, the bench has become a cherished landmark within the community, a symbol of continuity amidst the ever-changing landscape of human lives. It is a testament to the moments of joy, sorrow, and reflection experienced by those seeking its comfort. Couples have whispered sweet nothings under the blanket of stars, cementing their love in the quiet solitude it offers. Friends have reunited, their laughter pealing across the water, rekindling bonds that time nor distance could sever. Even in solitude, the bench provides companionship, its steadfast presence a reminder that one is never truly alone.

With its unspoken stories, this bench by the lake encapsulates the essence of connection that threads through the fabric of our existence. It mirrors the myriad facets of human emotion and interaction, where the simple act of sitting and being can open the door to profound experiences.

It reminds us that amidst the hustle of daily life, there exist sanctuaries of peace and connection, spaces that hold the potential to transform our understanding of the world and our place within it.

As twilight descends, casting a golden hue over the lake, the bench remains a beacon for those seeking peace, a sliver of beauty, or the warmth of shared experience. It is a silent witness to the tapestry of human life, a testament to the enduring nature of simple spaces that hold profound significance in our lives. In its simplicity, the bench by the lake invites us to embrace the moments of connection available to us to cherish the stories and lives that intersect in the most ordinary places.

In this narrative of connection and reflection, the bench by the lake emerges not merely as an object within a landscape but as a character in its own right, a keeper of stories and a facilitator of human experience. It serves as a reminder that within the framework of our daily lives, spaces exist imbued with the potential for meaningful interaction, solace, and inspiration. As we move forward, let us carry with us the lessons of the bench by the lake—the beauty of simplicity, the richness of shared moments, and the enduring strength of the bonds we forge with one another and the world around us.

CHAPTER 16

THE SYMPHONY OF THE EVERYDAY

In the tapestry of daily life, moments that resonate with the symphony of the every day often go unnoticed, like the soft hum of a distant melody. Yet, within these instances, the essence of life's joy and familial bonds are deeply woven. One such moment, making breakfast, transforms from a routine task into an arena of laughter, competition, and connection, illustrating the profound impact of sharing simple activities. This chapter delves into the heart of these moments, starting with a tradition that turns the kitchen into a stage for family dynamics to unfold in the most delightful ways.

16.1 THE GREAT PANCAKE FLIP-OFF

Flipping Tradition

Imagine a Sunday morning where the scent of brewing coffee blends with the aroma of batter on a hot griddle. Here, a family gathers to share a meal and partake in a tradition that elevates breakfast to a spectacle of joy and friendly rivalry. The Great Pancake Flip-Off, an event marked not by its grandeur but by its ability to draw laughter and cheer, becomes a testament to how traditions can enrich family life, no matter how small. With each flip, a pancake soars, an embodiment of the light-hearted competition that infuses the morning with excitement.

Unexpected Techniques

In this culinary contest, the spatula becomes a wand, granting those who wield it the power to attempt gravity-defying feats with their pancakes. Techniques vary, from the scientifically calculated angle of the flip to the more whimsical, such as adding a jump for momentum. Tools are modified for the occasion; spatulas are taped to the ends of broomsticks for extra leverage, and non-stick pans are greased with meticulous care to ensure the perfect launch. This improvisation and creativity underscore the joy of adapting everyday tasks into opportunities for play and laughter.

Breakfast Blunders

With high stakes come high-flying pancakes—and the occasional misfire. Pancakes adorn the ceiling, stick to the walls, or land with a splat on the floor in a moment of ill-timed coordination, much to the delight of the family dog, who has learned that mornings like these promise unexpected treats. These blunders, far from deterring the competition, add layers of hilarity to the tradition, reminding all involved of the beauty in imperfection and the shared joy in recovery and laughter following each failed flip.

The Heart of the Home

As the last pancake lands (successfully or not) on a plate and the family settles around the table, reflections on the morning's escapades turn to discussions about upcoming events, personal victories, and challenges. This transition from competition to connection highlights the kitchen's role as the heart of the home, a place where meals are made, but more importantly, where memories are crafted. The Great Pancake Flip-Off, in its essence, is more than a tradition; it's a catalyst for bonding, an invitation to engage in the present moment fully, and a reminder of the strength and warmth found in the shared experiences of family life.

Visual Element: A Flip in Time

A series of photos captures the essence of The Great Pancake Flip-Off, from the concentration on faces as pancakes are flipped to the inevitable laughter that follows the less successful attempts. These images, paired with captions detailing the thought process behind each technique and the reactions to each outcome, offer a visual narrative of the tradition. Accompanying the photos, a pancake recipe encourages readers to start their version of the Flip-Off, fostering new traditions and memories.

In this symphony of the every day, where the mundane transforms into moments of connection and joy, the Great Pancake Flip-Off stands as a testament to the power of shared traditions. It reminds us that within the ordinary lies the extraordinary, waiting to be uncovered through laughter, competition, and the warmth of family bonds. As we move through the tapestry of daily life, let us remember to cherish these moments, for it is in them that the essence of life's joy and the depth of our connections indeed unfold.

16.2 THE DAY THE GROCERY LIST GOT SWITCHED

On an overcast afternoon, where whispers of an impending rainstorm mingled with the mundane, two neighbors, unbeknownst to each other, set the stage for an inadvertent culinary caper. Their grocery lists, meticulously penned to nourish their households for the week, became entangled in a comedy of errors. A swift gust of wind, capricious in its aim, seized these scrolls of sustenance from their hands, swapping their destinies as neatly as a stage magician's sleight. In this moment of innocent confusion, the foundation for

an unexpected journey into the world of gas-
tronomy was laid.

In the aisles of the local supermarket, where the
array of produce and goods stretched as far as the
eye could see, our protagonists

Found themselves adrift in a sea of unfamiliar
ingredients. The lists they clutched, now foreign
scripts in their hands, spoke of items neither
had encountered in their culinary expeditions.
Exotic fruits whose names danced awkwardly
on their tongues, and canned goods that
promised flavors uncharted, beckoned with a
siren's call.

Amidst the linoleum tiles and fluorescent lights,
it was here that bewilderment gave birth to curiosity, transforming a routine chore into an adventure.

As baskets filled with these peculiar provisions,
the stage was set for an evening of unexpected
creations. Kitchens, once arenas of routine
recipes, transformed into laboratories of taste,
where the unfamiliar ingredients whispered secrets of distant lands. A fruit, vibrant and alien in
its appearance, revealed a sweetness that sang of
sun-kissed orchards, while a tin of mysterious

contents unveiled flavors that spoke of ancient culinary traditions.

Though born from confusion, each dish carried within it the essence of discovery, turning dinner tables into gateways to unseen worlds.

The outcomes of this serendipitous mixups were as varied as they were delightful. Meals planned with precision gave way to dishes that defied convention, where the tang of an unknown spice could elevate a simple stew to a masterpiece.

Once predictable in their comfort, Snacks became exotic treats that teased the palate with unfamiliar textures and flavors. It was in these moments of shared meals that the true magic of the mixup revealed itself, not in the novelty of the ingredients, but in the connections they forged.

Laughter, a melody as ancient as time, filled their homes, its cadence rising and falling with the tales of their culinary misadventures.

Stories of bafflement at the supermarket, tentative first bites, and dishes gone hilariously awry wove a tapestry of camaraderie between the two households. This laughter, born from the acceptance of life's little mixups, served as a reminder of the joy that resides in life's unpredictability. It was a laughter that spoke of the resilience of the human spirit, of its capacity to find humor and happiness in the face of confusion.

As the sun dipped below the horizon, casting a golden glow that promised the storm's end, reflections on the day's events became softer. The mixup at the supermarket, a trivial mishap in the grand scheme of life, had unwittingly become a catalyst for exploration, for growth, and for connection. It underscored the beauty of stepping into the unknown, embracing the ingredients life offers, no matter how unfamiliar, and the richness of sharing these experiences with others.

The lessons were manifold in this narrative, where a simple switch of grocery lists became the prologue to a journey of culinary and personal discovery. In the face of life's unexpected turns, flexibility emerged not as a skill but as an art form, a dance with chance that can lead to the most delightful of outcomes. Humor, the golden thread that binds us in our shared humanity, proved once again to be a balm for the soul, turning potential frustration into an opportunity for laughter and connection.

As we close this chapter, let us carry forward the reminder that within the mundane lies the potential for magic, that in every mixup, there lies an opportunity for discovery, and that the meals we share are more than just sustenance—they are invitations to connect, to laugh, and to explore the boundless possibilities that life offers. In these shared moments, these unexpected journeys into the world of taste and companionship, we find the true essence of living—a celebration of the unpredictable, the unknown, and the joyously unplanned.

CHAPTER 17

A SYMPHONY OF MISHAPS AND MIRTH

The midst of life's orchestrated routines lies an unpredictable cadence, a series of notes strung together not by design but by the whimsical hands of fate. Within this melody, we find the essence of human connection, laughter, and the shared absurdities that bind us. This chapter unfurls one such tale, a narrative so steeped in the communal spirit and the hilarity of unintended consequences that it transcends the ordinary. It becomes a testament to the joy in life's unplanned orchestrations.

17.1 THE JELL-O MOLD THAT TOOK OVER THE NEIGHBORHOOD COOKOUT

A Culinary Experiment

Imagine, if you will, a sun-drenched afternoon, the air filled with the sizzle of grilling meat and the murmur of anticipation. Here, in the heart of a vibrant neighborhood, an idea took root—one that promised to meld culinary ambition with the charm of communal celebration. The task was seemingly simple: to craft a Jell-O mold of such grandeur that it would become the centerpiece of the annual neighborhood cookout. This feat would etch this year's gathering into the annals of local lore. With a recipe in hand, borrowed from a well-thumbed cookbook, the endeavor began, not in the vast confines of a professional kitchen but within the modest bounds of a home, where ambition often outpaces reality.

Growing Gelatin

As the mixture began to set, it became apparent that this was no ordinary Jell-O mold. The proportions, perhaps misread or miscalculated in the throes of culinary fervor, had birthed a creation that seemed to defy the laws of physics and kitchen counters alike. It grew, inch by inch until the refrigerator could no longer contain its burgeoning mass. Laughter bubbled up as the realization set in: the Jell-O mold had taken on a life of its own, expanding beyond the bounds of expectation into a gelatinous behemoth that threatened to eclipse the cookout itself.

Community Effort

In a twist that could only be described as serendipitously fitting, the neighborhood rallied, turning what could have been a culinary disaster into a spectacle of collective ingenuity. Kiddie pools, previously the domain of splashing children and lounging pets, became vessels to contain the jiggling giant. Bathtubs long resigned to the mundane task of cleanliness, found new purpose as molds for the overflow. The scene, reminiscent of a well-orchestrated comedy, unfolded under the golden hue of the setting sun, transforming the cookout into an event marked not by the food on the grill but by the communal dance of problem-solving and laughter.

Laughter and Legacy

In the aftermath, plates filled with slices of the now-tamed Jell-O mold, laughter continued to ripple through the assembly. Conversations meandered from the absurdity of the day's events to reflections on past gatherings, each tale spun with the thread of humor and the warmth of shared experience. In its unwieldy grandeur, the Jell-O mold had become more than a culinary centerpiece; it was a monument to the unpre-dictable beauty of life's mishaps and the joy they can bring when met with laughter and a sense of community. It stood as a testament to the idea that sometimes, the most memorable moments stem not from meticulous planning but from the chaotic symphony of life, played out in the key of spontaneity.

Visual Element: The Gelatinous Chronicle

An infographic, "The Gelatinous Chronicle," cap-tures the saga in vibrant hues and whimsical il-lustrations. From the initial ambitious stirrings of the culinary experiment to the community's in-ventive containment efforts, each phase of the Jell-O mold's journey is depicted, inviting readers to partake in the laughter and camaraderie that defined the day. Accompanying the visual narra-tive, a sidebar encourages readers to share their tales of culinary misadventures or communal tri-umphs, weaving their stories into the larger ta-pestry of shared human experience.

In this chapter, the melody of mishaps and mirth plays out against the backdrop of a neighborhood cookout, a setting as familiar as it is ripe for the unexpected. It reminds us that within every over-ambitious culinary endeavor, every misread recipe lies the potential for laughter, connection, and memories long after the last bite has been savored. In these moments, these spontaneous gatherings of friends and neighbors, we find the authentic flavor of the community, seasoned not just with salt and sugar but with the sweetness of shared joy and the savory notes of collective endeavor.

I Hope You Enjoyed a Good Laugh!

Thank you for choosing "107 Short Humorous Life Stories for Seniors"! I hope that each story brought you not only a smile but also kindled delightful memories and conversations.

Your feedback is incredibly important to me and to other readers who are considering this book. I would be grateful if you could take a few minutes to share your thoughts on Amazon. Your review could help others decide whether this book is right for them!

How to Leave a Review:

1. Visit the product page on Amazon.
2. Scroll down to the "Customer Reviews" section.
3. Click on "Write a customer review."
4. Rate the book and write your thoughts.

Alternatively, you can use your smartphone to scan the QR code below to be taken directly to the review page:

Or, if you prefer, click on the following link:
https://amzn.to/3V6U776

Thank you for your time and for helping us and your fellow readers. We look forward to hearing your thoughts!

CONCLUSION

Well, my dear reader, here we stand (or sit, or recline—no judgment here) at the end of a rather splendid journey, having traipsed through 107 stories that have, I hope, tickled your funny bone, warmed your heart, and perhaps made you see the seniors in your life through a kaleidoscope of laughter, nostalgia, and admiration. Together, we've navigated the highs and lows of everyday life, proving that humor is not just the best medicine. Still, the spoonful of sugar helps the reality sandwich go down.

As I hope you've gathered, these tales are far more than a mere collection of chuckles and guffaws. They celebrate resilience, creativity, and that indomitable spirit of mirth that only magnifies with age. They serve as a gentle nudge, reminding us all to peer into the rearview mirror of life with a smile while charging ahead with a sense of eager anticipation for the stories yet to unfold.

But let's remember the real MVPs of our stories: the seniors. These paragons of wit and wisdom have repeatedly shown us the importance of laughter, the richness of history, and the unparalleled depth of their knowledge. They are more than just the keepers of our collective past; they are vibrant, dynamic participants in the ongoing story of our lives, teaching us that the art of storytelling (and story-listening) is what indeed weaves the fabric of our connections.

I urge you, dear reader, to lean in closer to the seniors in your orbit. Listen to their tales, share a giggle or two, and maybe share a story of your own. Remember, storytelling is not just about preserving history; it's a bridge between generations, a lifeline that keeps the spirit of humor and camaraderie alive and kicking.

As we turn the final page on this compendium of laughter and memory, let's not view it as an ending but as an invitation—an invitation to embrace the lighter side of life, find joy in the mundane, and cherish the memories we forge along the way. I encourage you to revel in the stories nestled within these pages and venture out and create your own narratives, peppered with humor and steeped in the rich tea of life.

A hearty thank you for accompanying me on this rollicking ride. It's been an absolute pleasure to share these stories with you. I hope they've sparked a flame of joy, curiosity, and perhaps a newfound appreciation for the seniors in your life. Carry forward the torch of storytelling and laughter, for in doing so, we bridge time and age, fostering bonds that are both timeless and priceless.

And finally, I'm all ears (figuratively speaking, of course)! I'd love to hear your thoughts on our shared journey, hear any humorous anecdotes about the seniors in your life, or hear how this book has reshaped your perspective on the older generation. Your feedback, stories, and reflections are the lifeblood of this ongoing adventure. Let's continue to foster a community built on the foundations of storytelling, laughter, and an unwavering appreciation for the seniors who enrich our lives in ways we can only begin to imagine.

Here's to many more stories, laughs, and an endless reservoir of memories. Cheers, my friend, to the symphony of mishaps and mirth that makes life worth living.

REFERENCES

The Best Senior Jokes and Funny Stories https://www. suddenlysenior.com/best-senior-jokes-book/

The Future of Hearing Aid Technology - PMC - NCBI https:// www.ncbi.nlm.nih.gov/pmc/articles/PMC4111503/

Lost and found glasses story (funny) https://www.alldeaf.com/ community/threads/lost-and-found-glasses-story-funny. 92472/

The effect of humor on short-term memory in older adults https://pubmed.ncbi.nlm.nih.gov/24682001/

Funny stories of parents and grandparents misusing tech https://www.upworthy.com/funny-stories-of-older-gener ations-using-technology

Intergenerational communication https://www.kontextor. org/en/blog/intergenerational-communication-how-to- communicate-effectively-across-generations/

7 True Stories About Funny Thanksgiving Mishaps https:// www.rd.com/list/true-stories-about-funny-thanksgiving- mishaps/

120+ Teen Slang Terms: 2024 Guide For Parents - Axis.org https://axis.org/resource/a-parent-guide-to-teen-slang/

RV Travel Tips for Seniors | Sixty and Me https://sixtyandme. com/senior-rv-travel-tips/

Golf Cart Safety Fact Sheet - Texas Department of Insurance https://www.tdi.texas.gov/pubs/videoresource/ fsgolfcart.pdf

Health Benefits of Gardening for Seniors https://www.lssliv ing.org/news/resources/health-benefits-of-gardening-for- seniors/

How to create a great community in a retirement village

https://www.plusscommunities.com/blog/retirement-community-belonging

1970s Disco Fashion: Bell-Bottoms And Boogie Shoes https://groovyhistory.com/1970s-disco-fashion

Jell-O Salad History: The Rise and Fall of an American Icon https://www.seriouseats.com/history-of-jell-o-salad

Dance Fever https://nostalgiacentral.com/television/tv-by-decade/tv-shows-1970s/dance-fever/

Remember Bell-Bottoms? History Of Flares Worn ... https://groovyhistory.com/bell-bottoms-history-of-flares-hippie-fashion

A Penny Saved: Thrift Bears Name Of A Founding Father | OCC https://www.occ.treas.gov/about/who-we-are/history/1863-1865/1863-1865-a-penny-saved.html

Why handwritten letters mean so much https://college.unc.edu/2023/11/why-handwritten-letters-mean-so-much/

Leisure and Entertainment in the Early Twentieth Century https://dcc.newberry.org/?p=16464

The Soap Box Derby | History https://www.smithsonianmag.com/history/the-soap-box-derby-94001863/

Nebraskans react to the moon landing, July 20, 1969, https://history.nebraska.gov/nebraskans-react-to-moon-landing-july-20-1969/

Elvis impersonator https://en.wikipedia.org/wiki/Elvis_impersonator

Technology that changed us: The 1990s, from ... https://www.zdnet.com/article/technology-that-changed-us-the-1990s/

Before Television: Childhood - Grandparents https://familytreevideo.com/before-television/

The Effects of Laughter Therapy on General ... https://www.ncbi.nlm.nih.gov/pmc/articles/PMC4280555/

The Surprisingly Violent, Rage-Filled World Of Bingo https://

www.cracked.com/personal-experiences-2542-the-surpris ingly-violent-rage-filled-world-bingo.html

Through the folk art of quilting, Tracy Vaughn-Manly works to ... https://news.weinberg.northwestern.edu/2023/02/ 14/tracy-vaughn-manly-works-to-preserve-quilting-his tory-at-northwestern/

Secret Language: Cryptography & Secret Codes https://www. exploratorium.edu/explore/secret-language

12 Funny Stories About Family Reunions! https://notal waysright.com/12-funny-stories-about-family-reunions/ 239487/

18 Biggest Baking Mishaps and How To Avoid Them https:// www.aol.com/food/18-biggest-baking-mishaps-and-how-avoid-them/

5 Amazing Stories of Things Lost, Then Found https://www. rd.com/list/5-amazing-stories-of-things-lost-then-found/

The Importance of Family Connections for Healthy Aging https://atlasseniorliving.com/the-goldton-at-st-peters burg/2023/04/20/the-importance-of-family-for-healthy-aging-a-guide-to-stronger-connections/

The health benefits of humor https://mcpress.mayoclinic.org/ healthy-aging/the-health-benefits-of-humor/

Powerful and deadly: The most severe blizzards in US history https://www.washingtonpost.com/weather/2022/12/22/ worst-blizzards-us-history/

Charting the Course for Senior Athletes https://growing bolder.com/stories/charting-the-course-for-senior-athletes/

Positive aging benefits of home and community gardening ... https://www.ncbi.nlm.nih.gov/pmc/articles/PMC6977207/

It Has Come to My Attention That You're Doing Karaoke ... https://slate.com/human-interest/2023/07/karaoke-songs-rules-etiquette-guide-right-wrong.html

Why Museums are Important for Seniors https://www.maple woodseniorliving.com/blog/why-museums-are-impor tant-maplewood-senior-living/

16 Short Funny Travel Stories That'll Make You Laugh Out ... https://jessieonajourney.com/short-funny-travel-stories/

Baby Boomer Travel Trends: More Trips, Richer Experiences https://www.sevencorners.com/blog/travel-tips/why- more-baby-boomers-are-opting-for-experiential-travel

How older people are mastering technology to stay connected after lockdown https://theconversation.com/how-older- people-are-mastering-technology-to-stay-connected-af ter-lockdown-165562

8 Reasons Seniors Can Struggle with Technology https:// www.helpcloud.com/blog/8-reasons-seniors-can-strug gle-with-technology/

The Benefits of Social Technology Use Among Older ... https://www.ncbi.nlm.nih.gov/pmc/ articles/PMC5312603/

Optimizing tech for older adults https://www.apa.org/moni tor/2021/07/tech-older-adults

Halloween Costume Contest - Best Fundraising Ideas https:// bestfundraisingideas.com/idea/halloween-costume- contest/

The Best Christmas Light Displays in Every State https:// www.travelandleisure.com/holiday-travel/best-christmas- lights-in-every-state

The Easter Egg Hunt - Short Kid Stories https://www.short kidstories.com/story/the-easter-egg-hunt/

Humor and Aging - A Mini-Review | Gerontology https:// karger.com/ger/article/59/5/448/147461/Humor-and- Aging-A-Mini-Review

Why Listening to Birds Boosts Mental Health - CASSY https://cassybayarea.org/why-listening-to-birds-boosts- mental-health/

40 Holidays Around The World To Celebrate Our Diversity ... https://www.boredpanda.com/holidays-around-the-world/

Non-human electoral candidates https://en.wikipedia.org/wiki/Non-human_electoral_candidates

The Role of Pets in Preserving the Emotional and Spiritual ... https://www.ncbi.nlm.nih.gov/pmc/articles/PMC9490679/

World's Greatest Grape Pie Contest https://naplesgrapefest.org/pie.php

The Challenges of Running a Community Theater https://blog.stageagent.com/challenges-of-running-a-community-theater/

Building Your Community Ties with a Block Party - SNEUCC.org https://www.sneucc.org/blogdetail/building-your-community-ties-with-a-block-party-12779969

Neighborhood Walking and Social Connectedness - NCBI https://www.ncbi.nlm.nih.gov/pmc/articles/PMC9062734/#:

The Psychology of Chance Encounters and Life Paths https://psycnet.apa.org/doiLanding?doi=10.1037/0003-066X.37.7.747

Missing Dog! – A Story about Distress, Support, and Community https://www.roamingabout.com/missing-dog-a-story-about-distress-support-and-community/

Revisiting the impact of public spaces on the mental health of ... https://ij-healthgeographics.biomedcentral.com/articles/10.1186/s12942-024-00365-8

The Unexpected Power of Random Acts of Kindness https://www.nytimes.com/2022/09/02/well/family/random-acts-of-kindness.html

The Effects of Laughter Therapy on General ... https://www.ncbi.nlm.nih.gov/pmc/articles/PMC4280555/

The History of American Breakfast https://www.voanews.

com/a/usa_all-about-america_history-american-break
fast/6172177.html

Parents Fed Their Kids Dog Treats After Grocery Store Mixup
https://www.vice.com/en/article/59z4qb/parents-fed-
their-kids-dog-treats-after-grocery-store-mixup

How To Cook With An Unfamiliar Ingredient https://summer
tomato.com/2009/04/27/how-to-cook-with-an-unfamil
iar-ingredient/

Jell-O Salad History: The Rise and Fall of an American Icon
https://www.seriouseats.com/history-of-jell-o-salad

A Brief History of the American Cookout https://food52.com/
blog/26334-history-of-the-american-cookout

Before Jell-O, Colorful Gelatin Desserts Were Haute Cuisine
https://www.atlasobscura.com/articles/invention-of-
gelatin-jello

Why older adults benefit from regular doses of humor https://
www.ama-assn.org/delivering-care/population-care/why-
older-adults-benefit-regular-doses-humor

Made in the USA
Monee, IL
01 October 2024

67015525R00144